POSITIVE
PROTESTANTISM

Euāgeliō (*that we cal gospel*) *is a*
greķe worde, and signyfyth good, mery,
glad and joyfull tydings, that maķeth a
mannes hert glad, and maķeth hym synge,
daunce and leepe for ioye.
— William Tyndale, *Prologue*
to the New Testament, 1525.

POSITIVE
PROTESTANTISM

An Interpretation of the Gospel

HUGH THOMSON KERR, JR., PH.D.

Professor of Systematic Theology
Princeton Theological Seminary
Princeton, New Jersey

Philadelphia
THE WESTMINSTER PRESS

CONTENTS

FOREWORD

THIS IS NOT an anti-Roman-Catholic book. And it is not a defense of Protestantism as such. It is written out of the conviction that the big issue before the Christian Church today is neither the controversy between Romanists and Protestants nor the justification of Protestantism as it now exists, but the prior and more basic question of the essence of the Christian faith.

The thesis of the book is that the essence of Christianity is to be found in the gospel — the good news that God was in Christ for man's redemption. It was the rediscovery of this gospel that provided the religious and spiritual dynamic of the Reformation in the sixteenth century. Protestantism, therefore, if it is to speak in our day with prophetic authority, must maintain, by reaffirming the gospel, that it is essential Christianity. This may, indeed, carry the implication that Protestantism is set against Romanism or its own contemporary existence, but the accent falls not so much on analysis of the present situation, whether Roman or Protestant, as upon the one thing needful — the recovery in our time of the gospel, with its full relevancy for faith and life.

The reaffirmation of the gospel demands a shift from the negative to the positive, from the defensive to the offensive, from the critical to the creative. That is the reason for speaking of *positive* Protestantism. It scarcely needs to be said that the adjective in this connection has nothing to do with the school of thought known as Positivism, which is associated with Auguste Comte and modern scientific naturalism. The word is used in the popular rather than the philosophical sense.

By "positive Protestantism" is meant nothing more, and also nothing less, than a straightforward, unequivocal proclamation of the gospel. What follows, consequently, is in the nature of a manifesto, an ultimatum, or, less grandly, a tract for the times. This explains, among other things, the brevity of the book and the almost complete absence of the academic impedimenta which usually appear in footnotes and bibliographical allusions of all kinds. It would have been an easy task to festoon nearly every page with a display of references to other books, but something is lost surely when an author feels he must be constantly authenticating and vindicating what he has to say by documenting his evidence as if he were being prosecuted before a court of law. Anyone who reads these pages will know how indebted they are to all sorts of men and books, and it hardly seemed to serve any useful purpose to underline the obvious.

It may be of interest to disclose some of the reasons that led to the preparation and development of the theme of this book. Quite specifically, it grew out of an elective course given to theological students, under the title "The Essence of Christianity." More and more it became apparent, however, that the question that Adolf von Harnack raised just fifty years ago — "What is Christianity?" — is an exclusively Protestant question and one that is being raised anew in our own day because of the widespread confusion as to what the Christian faith is all about. It is quite true, of course, that the question is as important, if not more so, for Roman Catholicism, but the point is that it has been raised and discussed mostly by Protestants.

Immediately after the war a number of recently discharged chaplains returned to the seminary campus to take some refresher courses, and several of these and other ex-GI's found their way into this particular classroom. They were quite frank in stating that what they wanted was not a polemic Protestantism or an analysis of the history of denominations or still less a theoretical discussion of doctrines and creeds. They had become, through their active war experience, somewhat critical of the traditional apologetic and at the same time deeply aware of the need for an authoritative and constructive approach to the whole question of the Christian faith. They were, of course, not hesitant in criticizing what they did not like about the course, but they also indicated real satisfaction with the emphasis upon the gospel as the heart and core of Christianity. It was largely because of their honest appreciation, and the added thought that in their quest they were perhaps more typical than they knew of countless other seekers in our day, that the following chapters gradually took shape.

The argument of the book may be briefly stated. It begins with an analysis of " The Plight of Protestantism " (Chapter One) which, in a word, is the evident confusion and ambiguity as to what it stands for. This perplexing and intolerable situation is aggravated by the fact that Protestantism is inherently critical of itself. The ecumenical movement has brought a new sense of unity and purpose, and yet even at this point Protestantism's unrest is evident because of the ambiguity between an emerging ecumenicity that seeks to transcend traditional differences and Protestantism's historic tie to the Reformation and its subsequent forms. In order to understand its own genius, therefore, Protestantism must re-examine its historical roots in the sixteenth century.

The Reformation dynamic is seen to be " A Deeper Plunge

Into the Gospel" (Chapter Two). This means that Protestantism cannot be properly understood as a sixteenth century variety of Christianity, but that its roots are deep within the New Testament. This calls for an investigation of "The Gospel in Christianity" (Chapter Three). The gospel, as a theological exegesis of the word itself shows, is the good news that God was in Christ for man's redemption. It was this that the Reformers rediscovered in their day, and it is this that is needed for the re-creation of contemporary Protestantism.

What the reaffirmation of the gospel would mean for present-day Protestantism is considered, first, in terms of the proclamation of the gospel message, or "The New Preaching of the Gospel" (Chapter Four), and secondly, in relation to the communication of the gospel, or "The Evangelistic Perspective" (Chapter Five). In the light of what has been said about Protestantism and the gospel, an epilogue, "The Tomorrow of Protestantism" (Chapter Six), is addressed to the related questions of the Church, the character of the Christian life, and the prospect for the future of Protestantism.

The Plight of Protestantism

Protestantism as a church *for the masses can continue to exist only if it succeeds in undergoing a fundamental change.* . . . *To continue to live, it must reformulate its appeal so that it will provide a message which a disintegrated world seeking reintegration will accept. It has to remold its forms of life, its constitution, its rites, and its individual and social ethics. But the precondition for any readjustment is that the Protestant leaders become aware of the seriousness of their situation.*

CHAPTER ONE

THE WORLD is on pilgrimage. We are not sure of the shrine to which we journey, but we are sure that the place where we are now is not the place where we should be. We know that we cannot go on at this slow pedestrian rate, for to go on as we are is not to go *on* at all. We do not know if civilization is going forward or backward, but we know that we are on the march. This is essentially true of our political and economic world, and we do not know if the confusion in which we find ourselves is a portent of disaster or the darkness before the dawn. The historian has taken up the problem, but his analysis is ambiguous and uncertain. We are like wanderers in our world — the sun gone down, darkness over us, our rest a stone. Unlike the wanderer of old, however, we do not yet see the vision, but we are questing, groping, and peering into the gloom.

It is little wonder that religion should partake of this restless pilgrim spirit. The religions of the world are conscious of their transcendence over the shifting problems of space and time, and yet they are bound up with the confusion of the times. Nearly every great religious movement, whether of antiquity or of modern times, is in the process of change, adjustment, and reform. Recent studies in comparative re-

The quotation on the facing page is from *The Protestant Era*, page 229, by Paul Tillich. Copyright, 1948, by The University of Chicago Press. Used by permission.

ligion stress the revolution that is taking place in the older beliefs. All religions are acutely self-conscious and realize that a new dynamic must be discovered if they are to command respect and offer a prophetic vision for our day.

The Christian religion takes its place along with other religions of the world in experiencing the restless revolutionary spirit of our day. The Orthodox Church stands at the crossroads, and no one knows which road it will take tomorrow. The proud affluent Church of the czars has disappeared never to return, and although the resurgence of the Russian Church in recent years gives some cause for hope, there is also cause for alarm, for Christianity cannot be true to itself if fettered and bound by the restrictions and requirements of a totalitarian State. The Roman Catholic Church has set itself against this encroaching revolution from the East, but in doing so it has found itself involved in other, perhaps more perilous, positions. United in its denunciation of Communism and sure of its own authority, Roman Catholicism has found itself making necessary adjustments in its own provinces — in Italy, in Spain, in Poland, in Czechoslovakia, in Hungary, in South America.

The plight of Protestantism is in some ways simply commensurate with the plight of Christendom, the non-Christian religions, and the complex civilization of our day. The pilgrim quest is apparent in Protestantism as in other religions. The spirit of restlessness, the felt need for inner renewal and reform, the necessity for relating itself to contemporary concerns are all self-evident characteristics of contemporary Protestantism. The plight of Protestantism, speaking in general terms, is simply the plight of the world in which we live. It is a plight shared by Roman Catholicism, Eastern Orthodoxy, and the great non-Christian religions, and the plight of religion in general is but one aspect of the plight of the modern world. This means that the problem that confronts Protestantism today is related to the problem facing our whole contemporary civilization.

THE PRINCIPLE OF PROTEST

There is, however, something peculiarly Protestant about the restlessness of our day. Protestantism, as the name itself suggests, contains an inner principle of protest which gives it, like no other religious or social movement, a self-critical frame of mind. This principle of protest is the strength of Protestantism in so far as it becomes the source of prophetic and creative insights that result in inner renewal and reformation. It is also the weakness of Protestantism in so far as this principle of protest turns in upon itself in a merely negative and reactionary way, issuing in an uneasy conscience and the paralyzing fear of ultimate bankruptcy. Consequently, the plight of Protestantism is in a unique way commensurate, not only with the world in which we live, but with its own essence.

Protestantism in so far as it gives expression to the principle of protest can never be self-satisfied, for it is essentially self-critical. It is not merely that Protestantism protests against whatever it takes to be false and misleading; Protestantism protests against itself. It is this attitude of *self-*criticism that sets Protestantism over against all other religions. The religion of the Moslems, for example, may be in the throes of a reform movement, seeking to emancipate the living heart of the Koran from the shackles of an ancient civilization, but it is not generally characterized by radical self-criticism of its own essential mission and purpose. Roman Catholicism may be in the midst of a vigorous assault upon atheistic Communism, but it is not in the least self-critical of its own message. Protestantism, however, is uneasy, not only because of the plight of the world, but because it is conscious of an inner plight occasioned by its own tendency toward self-examination.

Wherever Protestantism is consciously critical of itself, this may be taken as a good omen and a healthy symptom, for the possibility of renewal depends upon the willingness of Protestantism to protest against itself. The *possibility* of renewal, we say, for it is not inevitable that radical self-criticism will of itself issue in reform or rebirth. It is because reformation is only a possibility and not a certainty that the plight of Protestantism is a peril. The peril makes itself felt when self-criticism is so radical as to frustrate all hopes for transformation. This becomes a real threat when self-criticism is aimless, ambiguous, or unable to discover the true source of its protest. Self-examination is not a hopeful sign in itself because it may result in confusion and rout. This is the risk that Protestantism runs when it turns the principle of protest in upon itself, and unless it can discover through such a self-scrutiny how it must be reformed, the possibility of rebirth will be forfeited.

PROTESTANTISM'S NEGATIVE BURDEN

The big issue confronting contemporary Protestantism is the necessity for redeeming what we have called the inner principle of protest from its association with sheer negativism. So long as Protestantism understands itself as no more than a protest movement in reaction to what it regards as falsehood and error, it stands in peril of its very existence. Only if Protestantism can become positive is there hope for its future.

There is no doubt that Protestantism at the present time suffers from a negative affliction. The word itself carries with it negative associations. Historically it comes from the Diet of Spires in 1529, when a protest was lodged against the attitude of the Roman Church toward the Lutherans. This relation of antagonism and opposition between the Roman Church and the Reformation gave to Protestantism a reactionary character which it has never completely transcended. For this reason Protestantism is usually defined as over against Roman Catholicism in such a way as to make it appear that the former is a negative reaction to the latter. A Protestant, so the dictionary tells us, is a member or adherent of any Christian Church or body severed from Rome, and Protestantism is defined as the religion of those who are opposed to Roman Catholicism.

Such a negative interpretation puts Protestantism at a distinct disadvantage when it tries to say exactly what it believes. The Roman Church is quite well aware of this Protestant predicament and makes the most of its own positive authoritarianism. This has accentuated the uneasy conscience of Protestantism. The resurgent Romanism of our day, with all its characteristic aggressiveness, is being confronted by a Protestantism whose only weapon of attack is to protest. This means that Protestantism is put on the defensive; it is fighting a rear-guard action. It is clear that Protestantism must combat Romanism with something more than a negative protest, and it must understand itself to be something more than a non-Roman sectarian movement.

The Roman issue, however, is only one aspect of Protestantism's present dilemma and perhaps not the most important at that. The negative stamp which Protestantism has acquired because of its opposition to Rome has spread like a disease throughout the whole structure of Protestantism, enervating its power and sapping its vitality. Protestants are becoming acutely conscious of their negativism, not simply because historically they are in reaction to Rome, but because

it is so difficult to know precisely what is the positive mission
and message of Protestantism. It is this lack of positive conviction that constitutes the lurking peril of sheer negativism
and serves to distinguish contemporary Protestantism from
the period of the Reformers.

Negative reaction may be a justifiable and necessary corol-
lary of what we have called Protestantism's inner principle
of protest. It may be that in a unique way Protestantism by
its very nature must take up a negative and reactionary position, not only against Rome but against itself. Certainly the
Reformers were unsparing in their criticisms of Rome and
even of themselves. But the difference is that Luther and
Calvin, for example, knew very well *why* they were protesting, whereas that is just what contemporary Protestantism does not know. Negative reaction by itself, in other
words, is not necessarily a sign of confusion or lack of positive conviction. The logician tells us that every negative implies a positive, that it is impossible to deny without also
affirming, and so we are justified in saying that behind the
original Protestant revolt there was something more than
negation. The negation was in fact the result of an inner
conviction.

It was because of what the Reformers *believed,* and not
because of what they *denied* that Protestantism came into
being. Their positive belief was so strong that they were unable to tolerate what in their view was manifestly erroneous
and corrupt. The inner principle of protest which inspired
the Reformers did not result in sheer negativism for the
simple reason that it was motivated, not by a captious critical
spirit or a sense of inner confusion, but by a definite assurance that to them had been given the needed insight into
divine truth. It was because they were self-consciously positive about what they believed that they were also radically

reactionary in their attitude toward Rome. It would be a mistake, therefore, to seek the essence of the Reformation in the fact of negative reaction against Romanism. This was simply a historical accident, the occasion for the Protestant revolt, and it cannot be properly understood merely in terms of reaction. The reaction, the negation, the revolt, the opposition — all this was the result and by-product of a positive faith.

Present-day Protestantism, however, has fallen victim to the charge that it is basically negative because it has lost sight of its positive presuppositions. The inner principle of protest has been deprived of its creative dynamic because it is no longer clear why or on what grounds Protestantism protests. This is the real peril of contemporary Protestantism, and not, for example, the Roman Catholic issue, because it implies a confusion and ambiguity about essential affirmations. The strength of Protestantism's protest depends upon the consciousness of a positive faith, and if this is lacking or in doubt, the initial impulse of Protestantism is obscured.

It is a hopeful sign that Protestants are becoming aware of the need for the recovery of just such a positive position. Recent books on the subject are taking special pains to point to the positive rather than the negative interpretation of Protestantism. We are reminded that the Latin word *protestari* has always meant " to profess " as well as " to protest," and allusion is made to Shakespeare and Samuel Johnson, both of whom used the word in its positive sense of public declaration. But something more is needed than technical recourse to the etymology of the word. It is not enough to assert that Protestantism has its positive side unless we know better than we now do what that position is.

Protestantism, even in its confusion about its own essence, however, has an advantage over other forms of religious thought by being able and willing to turn the principle of protest in upon itself. In this sense, Protestantism's uneasiness about itself is a valuable asset. It may, of course, simply issue in despair and further confusion, but it may also be the means by which the foundations are shaken in order to leave exposed those things that cannot be shaken. In any event, the very restlessness and disquiet of contemporary Protestantism is an indication of a groping after unshakable realities and an impatience with things as they are. The most obvious illustration of this groping mood, which shows both the negative and the positive side of the principle of protest, is the fact of Protestant disunity and the quest for an ecumenical consensus which may become the point of departure for a transformed and transforming Protestantism for our day.

DISUNITY AND THE ECUMENICAL HOPE

When Protestantism takes stock of itself, as it is doing today, it is acutely embarrassed by its own sectarian history and ashamed of its present disunity. There is little disposition at the present time to glory in the history of Protestant divisions. We speak disparagingly of the " proliferation of sects " and the " fissiparous tendency " of Protestantism. The older traditional loyalties have largely lost their hold. There are few denominational controversies and practically no evidence of the older polemic that divided group against group and engendered so much bad feeling. There is a growing impatience with Protestantism as sectarianism, and an increasing realization that it cannot hope to stand for anything positive so long as it is divided and rent asunder.

The measure of Protestantism's embarrassment at its own divisiveness is the rapid growth of the ecumenical movement within the present generation. As a phenomenon of modern

Church history, the ecumenical movement is a clear indication that Protestantism has ceased to be centrifugal and has now become centripetal. We are living in an age when individual Protestant denominations are coming together at an increasing rate. The broken fragments are being gathered together, Protestant history is reversing itself, and there is a distinct gravitation from the periphery to the center. Separated members of the same traditional families are reuniting, and the roll call of such family reunions is impressive. Although there have been some incidental schisms which mar the record, the main trend is unquestionably in the direction of closer co-operation and union.

All such efforts and successes, however, pale into insignificance in the light of the recently created World Council of Churches, which owes its primary significance to the fact that at Amsterdam in 1948 more than 150 Churches, most of them in the Protestant tradition, put themselves on record as favoring closer co-operation. The World Council is the most convincing instance we have yet seen of the swing of the pendulum from Protestant disharmony to Protestant unity. Whatever may be said of the past, it is no longer accurate to speak of Protestantism as essentially divisive, and there is evidence enough in recent history to suggest that it has entered a new era so far as denominational disunity is concerned.

But the ecumenical movement, whether on the national or international level, is not so reassuring as it ought to be, and Protestantism, true to its own nature, has even turned the principle of protest upon this otherwise desirable tendency toward unity. There is deep concern, even among those who most stoutly defend the ecumenical movement, lest the passion for unity be misdirected and misunderstood. It is doubtless an encouraging sign that Protestantism has ceased to glory in its divisions and seeks a more common meeting ground. But the question arises, " What is the basis for such unity, whence comes this passion, what constitutes the common denominator upon which Protestant unity can be built? " There are at least three possible answers to this question, two of which illustrate the plight of Protestantism in terms of self-criticism, while the third gives promise that the negative aspect of the principle of protest will give way to a more positive conception of ecumenicity.

There are those who advocate the ecumenical movement on strictly prudential and functional grounds. The argument here is quite simple, and in many ways compelling. Given the desire for unity which springs from the embarrassment of historical disunity, what better reason can be found for the ecumenical movement than the common concern to present a united front? Our world cries out for unity — " One world or none " is a slogan that has captivated the contemporary imagination — and what is so clearly necessary in the realm of economics and politics is equally applicable to the Christian Church. Isolationism, whether in international affairs or Church affairs, is a thing of the past. The choice laid upon us is an existential one — either we unite or we perish. National sovereignties may have to be surrendered, or at least held less dear than loyalty to the common purpose. The reason for all movements that look forward to greater unity is, in this sense, prudential and functional — we *must* unite if we are to exist.

So far as Protestantism is concerned, this ecumenical imperative comes with the force of an ultimatum. There is no possibility, for example, that the resurgent Romanism of our day can be met with successful resistance unless Protestantism can speak with one voice. Nor is there any hope that Protestantism can speak to the world if its witness is divided.

Whatever the differences of historical traditions may be, Protestantism must transcend these particular and individualistic sovereignties in the common search for a united front.

Although there are many who advance this pragmatic rationale for the ecumenical movement, it is significant that the World Council, for example, has taken special pains to guard against any such prudential or functional motivation for unity. The reason for this is obvious. The purpose of the ecumenical movement is not only to present a united Christian front, but to proclaim a united Christian message. And unless there *is* a united message, any organizational unity will be nothing more than a scaffolding, a façade, literally a "front." It is quite conceivable that the popular demand for a united Protestantism may result in a Church that has nothing to say. Such a unity would not be the outgrowth of a common faith or the by-product of an inner union; it would be a contrived and calculated unity undertaken for an ulterior purpose. The real purpose of ecumenicity is not merely to demonstrate *that* the Church is one, but *what* it is that constitutes its oneness.

A second approach to the problem of unity, which seeks to supply what the prudential view overlooks, suggests hopefully that once organizational unity is achieved, a common faith will result. That is to say, the *message* of the ecumenical movement will be the fruit rather than the root of unity. What a united Protestantism will have to say to the world will depend, first of all, upon its coming together. The testimony of such a united front cannot, therefore, be anticipated, and we ought not to prophesy in advance, for the simple reason that the common faith will be the by-product, and not the presupposition, of our oneness.

This argument draws heavily upon the prospect that an exchange of viewpoints, which the ecumenical movement makes possible, will produce in due course a new synthesis which will transcend the barriers of local traditions. This has, in fact, been the response of many to the first meeting of the World Council. That assembly has been hailed, not so much because it said anything unique, but because it was in itself a unique event. The message of the Council is in this way taken to be the fact that the Council was convened. We have been warned not to read too much into the official reports of the World Council, since the real message, we are told, is to be found in the event, and in what happens now that the concern for unity has found a formal medium for expression. This may be interpreted to mean that whatever ambiguities there are regarding a common faith, which the reports of Amsterdam themselves evidence, we can look forward to the possibility that now the Council has come into being a new consensus will gradually emerge. The real basis for unity will become apparent after the unity has been consummated.

To state the argument in this way, however, is to expose its patent deficiencies. This is clearly a case of putting the cart before the horse. What right have we to expect that where there is not now a common faith, a pooling of individual assets will produce one? Have we any right to say, "Look, we are united; we do not quite know why, but wait a little longer, and you will see that a common conviction will develop"? Do we have any evidence that this sort of thing actually happens?

Historically speaking, there is precedent against the sequence implied by this kind of reasoning. If the history of creeds and confessions means anything, it should teach us that unity is the result of common conviction, and not its cause. The classic creeds which have come down through the centuries came into existence because of a common faith.

Creeds do not precede, but presuppose, faith. It is because individuals, groups, or whole Churches *believe* something that they write creeds. While it is true that creeds and confessions of faith, particularly in the Reformation period, were often the formal expression of an agreed unity, the *unity* was not the cause of the statement of belief except in a formal way. A creed is simply a formal expression of a common conviction that already exists.

Unity, in other words, must be the result of a common faith. We must keep the sequence in its proper order: first the conviction, then the creed; first the inner consensus, then the outward unity. So far as a formal statement of belief is concerned, that may wait. But a unity that is not predicated on a common conviction is not likely *of itself* to produce one. We have no right to expect that the World Council, if it does not know on what common ground it has come into being, will itself create a common faith. The reason for its existence cannot be at the same time the product of its existence. It is not enough to come together for prudential reasons, and it is not realistic to start with unity in the hope that the basis of unity will by and by become self-evident.

There is, however, another and more constructive approach to the ecumenical movement which overshadows the two views just mentioned. We do not, so this position maintains, seek unity because it is required of us or because we hope a common conviction will be created, but because as a matter of fact there *is* an agreed unity of belief and faith. This would mean that the ecumenical movement, in so far as it is an attempt to establish an organizational unity, does so not in order to bring into existence what does not now exist, but in order to give expression to that measure of consensus which is already there. We unite, not to find our common agreement, but because of it. And what unites us is taken to be more important and basic than what divides us. Granting that uniformity may be a long way off or even undesirable, there is sufficient common ground at the present time to warrant a World Council of Churches. Such a Council has as its chief responsibility, therefore, not the formal demonstration of the oneness of the Church, or the creation of a common point of view which does not now exist, but the sole and single obligation of expressing that oneness which actually does unite the Churches.

From the published reports of the World Council, this would appear to be the point of departure that dominated the discussions at Amsterdam. There is a significant consistency about the way the various documents begin. For example, the first section of the report on " The Universal Church in God's Design " has to do with " Our Given Unity." This is expressed, in part, as follows: " God has given to His people in Jesus Christ a unity which is His creation and not our achievement. We praise and thank Him for a mighty work of His Holy Spirit, by which we have been drawn together to discover that, notwithstanding our divisions, we are one in Jesus Christ." The report on " The Church's Witness to God's Design " begins with a statement on " The Purpose of God," concerning which three " perfectly plain " propositions can be made: " All that we need to know concerning God's purpose is already revealed in Christ. It is God's will that the Gospel should be proclaimed to all men everywhere. God is pleased to use human obedience in the fulfillment of His purpose." The report on " The Church and the Disorder of Society," after stating the fact of social disorder, affirms that " the Christian Church approaches the disorder of our society with faith in the Lordship of Jesus Christ." The final section report, " The Church and the International Disorder," asserts: " God is not indifferent to misery or deaf to human prayer and aspiration. By accepting His Gospel, men will find forgiveness for all their sins and receive power to transform their relations with their fellow men. Herein lies our hope and the ground of all our striving."

What these brief extracts make clear is that it is possible to *begin* with unity. What the Church has to say on particular issues grows out of an agreed consensus and a basic Christian confession. The reports of Amsterdam, in this sense, may be said to mark a milestone, for they assume that there is a common faith which unites the Churches. The fact of the World Council is indeed a unique event, not merely because what Amsterdam *did* is more important than what Amsterdam *said,* but because the event was hailed by the Council itself as the expression of a unity in faith that already exists. It is true that we must not lay too much weight upon what Amsterdam said, since the first task of the World Council was, not to pontificate, but to consolidate. But it is equally dangerous to side-step the official reports and the unofficial discussions as if they were of secondary significance. In a real sense the event is revealed in the basic presuppositions of the reports. The Council could not have been a unique event if nothing had been said. If there had not been a sense of the common faith, the Council could not have become self-conscious or articulate. We must, of course, wait to see what the Council will *do* now that it has come into being, and we must wait to hear what it will *say* with a united voice, but one thing is already evident — the ecumenical movement at the present time does not merely talk about or look for unity; it regards itself as coming out of and speaking out of a unity that is there, so to speak, and only needs to be reaffirmed.

It is along this line and in this direction that there is hope for the renewal of that re-creative dynamic which was the source and motivation of original Protestantism. It is only when there is a basic unity of belief that there is prospect for a positive Protestantism. It will not come about so long as Protestantism remains on the defensive, content to protest or to raise a merely negative voice. It will not be achieved by forcing an external prudential unity upon confused and divided Churches; nor will it burst forth like spontaneous combustion once an organizational unity is achieved.

PROTESTANTISM AND THE CHRISTIAN CONSENSUS

It would be a mistake, however, to suggest that at long last the cure for the plight of Protestantism has been found in the creation of the World Council of Churches. Protestantism's negative proclivities, its confusion and ambiguity about what it stands for, its inability to rediscover the reason for its principle of protest — all this is not done away with because the World Council of Churches takes its departure from the conviction that there is a basic consensus of faith. The plight of contemporary Protestantism is due to the felt lack of such a consensus. In other words, the very thing that Protestantism lacks cannot at the same time be assumed or taken for granted as the acknowledged bond of unity. The point of departure for the Amsterdam documents, with all their stress on " our given unity," is the very thing that cannot be taken for granted. It may be that there is a deeper unity among the Churches, and especially within Protestantism, than has been apparent in modern times, but this is precisely what needs to be demonstrated.

It is not enough for the World Council of Churches to proclaim that a new basis of unity has been discovered, and that henceforth the Churches may proceed upon this common commitment. What *is* this essential agreement? What are its roots? Where does it come from? Why have we been so long in recognizing it? Questions such as these illustrate the fact that the plight of Protestantism is still with us. The World Council is the most tangible and encouraging evidence in our time that Protestantism is groping after a positive position, but it is not the end of the pilgrimage; it is only the beginning.

It is at this point that the plight of Protestantism is brought into sharp focus. For Protestantism has laid upon it not only the necessity of understanding and making articulate an agreed consensus of the faith; it must also relate this to itself in terms of its own historical self-consciousness. Protestantism is irrevocably associated with a historical context, namely, the Reformation of the sixteenth century and its subsequent development. Protestantism has a history; it can be dated as to time and place; it is possible to trace its roots back into a historical situation. The question arises, accordingly, " What has this historical reference to do with the search for and expression of a common Christian consensus of faith? " Or to put it another way, " What does the agreed point of departure as stated by the World Council have to do with Protestantism as a self-conscious historical phenomenon? "

It is clear that there are very different answers within Protestantism to this question. Those who seek ecumenicity in terms of the restoration of a broken unity, such as is supposed to have existed in the Early Church, are obviously more concerned with structural continuity than with the significance of a comparatively " late " revival movement such as the Reformation. Any such view as this necessarily undercuts the importance of Protestantism as a historical movement related to the sixteenth century. It may indeed consider itself as a mediating position between Rome and Wittenberg or Geneva, a "bridge Church" as many Anglicans would speak of it. But whatever merits this view may have in this respect, it tends to make Protestantism in its historical Reformation context unimportant and irrelevant.

At the other extreme stand those who would sacrifice a structural unity, the Anglican emphasis on apostolic succession for example, in favor of a doctrinal unity such as may be found in one or another of the Reformation creeds and confessions of faith. The emphasis here is upon pure doctrine, and this is in turn identified with some one aspect of the Reformation. This view is the opposite of the one just mentioned, for the reason that it consciously exalts the historical setting of Protestantism. The Reformation is not just a sixteenth century revival of religion; it is of epochal significance. Any talk of unity, therefore, must take into account the question of pure doctrine, and in so far as this type of Protestantism has developed into certain definite kinds of confessionalism, mainly Lutheran and Reformed or Calvinistic, there is a tendency to denominational or confessional absolutism.

Between these two extremes there is a third variety of Protestantism, which takes a somewhat indifferent or relativistic attitude toward the relation between historical Protestantism and the essential confession of the Church. Those who hold this view — for example, Baptists, Methodists, Quakers, Disciples, Congregationalists, and others — would be willing to acknowledge their historical origin in the Reformation, but they would not feel obligated in any way to pursue unity in terms of a sixteenth century conception of the faith. Differences in doctrine as well as Church government would be accepted with equanimity by all such, simply because they would take the multiplicity of Churches and confessions of faith to be the necessary and harmless expressions of an organic unity which, like the unity of the body, involves diverse and individualistic functions. This would make the Reformation confessions of faith of only relative value, and for this reason there is an obvious affinity between this view and the first — both deny that the Reformation was a unique historical phenomenon in the sense of providing a normative definition of Protestantism.

It would appear from these three types of contemporary Protestantism that, apart from a strict denominational and confessional creedalism, the Reformation is either being by-passed or is regarded as having exhausted itself. This is a conclusion, however, that many within Protestantism will not be persuaded to accept. The choice between a Protestantism that sits lightly to the Reformation and one that is restricted and limited to a particular kind of confessionalism is for many not a choice at all.

TOWARD A POSITIVE PROTESTANTISM

We believe there is a more positive and constructive interpretation of Protestantism which goes beyond the three types which have been mentioned. It is, in a word, what we choose to call positive Protestantism. It takes the Reformation seriously as the historical origin of Protestantism, but it sees the Reformation not merely as the occasion for the definition of pure doctrine but, in the fine phrase of Philip Schaff, as a deeper plunge into the meaning of the gospel itself. This means that the Reformation is important because it was the rediscovery of essential Christianity in the sixteenth century. Protestantism in this sense *is* Christianity, because it has the gospel at its core and center.

The analysis of contemporary Protestantism has gone far enough. We need something more than a diagnosis of the present ills of our diverse Churches and our different interpretations. If the principle of protest which characterizes Protestantism is not to lead to final despair and confusion, we must discover a positive Protestantism which will be true to its original historical impulses and at the same time true to essential Christianity. The search for such a positive Protestantism should be undertaken, not only for its own sake, but because it provides the clue to the relation between Protestantism and classic Christianity.

It may be that once again Protestantism is at the beginning of a radical reformation. It may be that through the centuries all the accumulating scholasticism and superstition, all the denominational bickering and sectarianism, have obscured the essence of the Christian gospel, as was the case in the days of the Reformers. The causes for this are, of course, different from those prevalent in the sixteenth century, but nonetheless it may be true that the essential message of the gospel has been forgotten or neglected. There is laid upon Protestantism, therefore, the responsibility of facing its contemporary plight and seeking a way out of the confusion and ambiguity which preclude the possibility of affirming a positive message. Once again we shall have to ask the question, " What is the gospel? " And in pursuit of this basic elemental question we may come to understand the true nature of positive Protestantism.

A Deeper Plunge Into the Gospel

The Reformation *of the sixteenth century is, next to the introduction of Christianity, the greatest event in history. . . . It was not a superficial amendment, not a mere restoration, but a regeneration; not a return to the Augustinian, or Nicene, or ante-Nicene age, but a vast progress beyond any previous age or condition of the Church since the death of St. John. It went, through the intervening ages of ecclesiasticism, back to the fountain-head of Christianity itself, as it came from the lips of the Son of God and his inspired Apostles. It was a deeper plunge into the meaning of the Gospel than even St. Augustine had made.*

CHAPTER TWO

O NE OF THE ENCOURAGING and significant movements within contemporary Protestantism is the renaissance of interest among historians and theologians in the meaning and purpose of the Reformation of the sixteenth century. There has always been a lively concern for the investigation of this revolutionary period of Church history, but at the present time we are witnessing a reassessment and reinterpretation which is in many ways unique and unparalleled. It is not only that new light has been shed on controversial problems, which is true enough. More important than this is the fact that contemporary scholarship is clearly informed by a revised and quite distinctive method of approach.

For some time we have been hearing of the " Luther research " movement which has been going on in Germany and in the Scandinavian countries, and the effects of this renaissance have been felt elsewhere. A less concerted but equally important effort has been made to reinterpret the Calvinistic and Reformed tradition, and there are evidences of a revival of interest in Zwingli, Bucer, Melanchthon, Bullinger, Cranmer, and Knox — the forgotten men of the Reformation. British scholars have been at work on their own complex Reformation history, and in America special atten-

The quotation on the facing page is from *The Creeds of Christendom,* Vol. I, page 204, by Philip Schaff. Sixth edition, 1931. Harper & Brothers.

tion has been given to the rise and subsequent influence of Anabaptist and other so-called "left-wing" Reformation groups.

It is difficult to estimate what the effect of this new scholarship will be upon the total evaluation of the Reformation, but it is already clear that in many respects traditional interpretations are being revised and in some instances radically modified. Ultimately this may require a rewriting of textbooks and histories of doctrine, but even more significant than this academic assignment will be the necessity for reforming our whole conception of the inner meaning of the Reformation itself.

What has been happening in recent years by way of fresh exploration of the Reformation may be briefly summarized under three major emphases. First, we are beginning to see more clearly than ever before that the Reformation cannot be understood merely by tracing the lines of historical, social, cultural, and economic development. Numerous attempts to do just this are, of course, useful in supplying background material for an age that is ever receding from us. But we cannot hope to understand Protestantism, either in its formative period or in its contemporary confusion, by trying to disentangle the threads of historical development.

We learn little about the Reformation dynamic by studying the influence of the Renaissance upon religion and learning, or by becoming aware of the expanding universe which science and geographical exploration opened up to the sixteenth century. The social, economic, and political conditions of the time are revealing factors in a total estimate of the Reformation, but they may easily leave untouched the spiritual, moral, and religious soul of the Protestant movement. The newer Reformation research is going beyond the quest for historical causes and is aware of the obligation to treat the Reformation as a specifically religious phenomenon. That is why there has been so much interest in the life and religious experience of the Reformers themselves and in the type of piety and devotion that characterized the times in which they lived. We are beginning to see that the clue to the Reformation lies more in the evangelical experience of those who were involved than in the impersonal and external changes of society and culture.

Another insight of the modern reading of the Reformation which follows upon what has just been mentioned is the growing recognition that Protestantism in its earliest and best representatives was conscious of reaffirming the apostolic gospel and quite innocent of any ambition to inaugurate a new religious movement. This means that we must radically revise our traditional Protestant interpretation of Church history. Not only must the Reformation period be seen as the literal re-formation of the sixteenth century in terms of the New Testament, but we must also be aware of the continuity between this classical reaffirmation and every other such reform movement during the interval between the first and the sixteenth century. Philip Schaff shocked some of his American friends in 1844 with the suggestion, contained in his Mercersburg inaugural lecture on "The Principle of Protestantism," that "the Reformation is the greatest act of the Catholic Church itself, the full ripe fruit of all its better tendencies." Recent scholarship has uncovered such tendencies in the medieval Church, and while this may seem to undercut some of the uniqueness of the Protestant revolt, it reminds us that the Reformers were the spokesmen of a continuous apostolic tradition. They made articulate what in previous generations was striving for expression.

A third feature of modern Reformation studies is the clear distinction made between the earliest years of the Reformation, the period of Luther and Calvin for example, and the later post-Reformation development of the seventeenth and eighteenth centuries. There is no doubt that in the generations succeeding the first flowering of the Reformation, a hoarfrost, as Brunner calls it, seems to have settled down upon the Protestant movement. The initial enthusiasm which swept all before it gave way to inner disputes and doctrinal polemics. The medieval scholasticism which the Reformers had so vehemently discarded came back with a vengeance to stifle and smother the essential affirmations of the Reformation. The controversial literature of these later years does not make edifying reading, and there is ample justification for calling this the age of Protestant scholasticism.

What makes this so important for our understanding of the soul of Protestantism is the fact that we have inherited much of this post-Reformation scholasticism through the standard traditional textbooks on theology and in many instances through the official creedal formularies of the larger denominations. And one reason for the plight of contemporary Protestantism is the justifiable reaction to this so-called Reformation tradition which is assumed to be an authentic expression of the thought and intention of the Reformers themselves. That it is, in fact, often a perversion or distortion of what the Reformation was all about is now becoming an established fact.

The interpretation of Protestantism that is needed at the present time is one that will take into account the newer insights into Reformation studies, three aspects of which we have briefly examined. At the risk of oversimplification, and as a sort of preface to a further study, we may venture such an interpretation in the form of a series of three propositions or theses.

THE REFORMATION WAS NOT SOMETHING NEW BUT SOMETHING OLD

Protestantism has for too long been burdened with the misunderstanding that it is a religious movement that began during the sixteenth century, and therefore a relatively late-comer in the history of the Christian Church. This is a deep-seated misconception which Roman Catholics in particular do their best to perpetuate, and they are often unwittingly aided by Protestants themselves. The official attitude of the Roman Church can be seen, for example, in question Number 160 of the Revised Edition of the Baltimore Catechism (1949), known as *A Catechism of Christian Doctrine* (No. 3). The question asks: " How do we know that no other church but the Catholic Church is the true Church of Christ?" And part of the answer reads: " Not one of the Christian sects can trace its origin to the apostles. . . . The Protestant churches began in the sixteenth century when their founders, rejecting certain doctrines of faith, broke away from Catholic unity."

If this were indeed the case, then Protestantism would have just cause for embarrassment. The denominations under such an interpretation would become not only competitors with each other but with Christianity itself. Protestantism cannot hope to speak in the name of essential Christianity so long as it marks its birthday with the sixteenth century. If it cannot be convincingly shown that the Reformation was, as Schaff maintained, in the direct line of every true reforming movement since the New Testament, then Protestantism must face the charge that it is not only new but novel and hence unable to substantiate its claim that it brought the medieval Church back to the apostolic Christian faith.

Protestants are themselves largely to blame for this mis-interpretation. A traditionally conservative denomination, for example, recently issued Sunday school materials in which a diagrammatic sketch was presented of the tree of Christianity. The roots of the tree are in the New Testament; the main trunk represents the Roman Catholic Church; the first major branch is the Eastern Orthodox Church; the second major branch is Protestantism which is further subdivided into hundreds of minor twigs and shoots. The net impression gained from such a diagram is that Protestantism is an offshoot from the central trunk of Christianity, a detour from the main highway, an aberration of the apostolic gospel.

Not all Protestant groups, of course, have been so easily misled about their history. The Episcopal and Anglican Churches, particularly the High or Anglo-Catholic traditions, have steadfastly refused to restrict themselves to what happened in the sixteenth century. The Tractarian Movement of the middle nineteenth century, commonly associated with John Henry Newman, had as one of its basic tenets the continuity of the English Church with apostolic beginnings. It was because Newman felt that this continuity was doubtful that he ultimately left the Church of England for the Church of Rome, but Anglicans have always maintained the continuity and make it support their own particular claims for the apostolic succession of their duly ordained clergy. For these and other reasons the Anglican Church likes to think of itself as a "bridge Church," a *via media,* spanning the chasm between Rome and other Protestant traditions.

There is no doubt that in their conception of historical continuity the Anglicans are absolutely right. The question of apostolic succession is not now before us, and we can dismiss that controversial issue with the remark that whatever we may think of the historical claim of the Anglican Church on this matter the idea of apostolic succession, especially of the succession of the apostolic gospel, is a soundly Protestant emphasis. The strange thing about the Anglican emphasis, however, is its reluctance to call itself Protestant, and its conviction that it alone preserves the line of apostolic continuity. This actually perpetuates in an indirect way the false and misleading charge that Protestantism is a late arrival and out of touch with apostolic Christianity, and that is why other Protestants often treat Anglicanism as a separate and distinct type of Christian witness, neither Roman nor Protestant.

Certain other Protestant groups, notably of the left-wing tradition, such as the Baptists and the Disciples, also vigorously assert their origin in the New Testament rather than in the sixteenth century. These groups, unlike the Anglicans, are not interested in problems of succession, and are much more self-consciously Protestant by temper and Reformational in theology. They have not succeeded, however, in uprooting the general impression among Protestants that the Reformation is really the historical point of departure, for they themselves cherish the Protestant label.

If we take the trouble to read the literature of the early years of the Reformation, we shall be forced to see how foreign to the minds of men like Luther and Calvin was the idea that Protestantism began in the sixteenth century. What they never tire of repeating is that they wish to introduce nothing new into the Church of their time; that their sole interest is the revival of New Testament Christianity; that, far from the Reformation's being an aberration, it is Rome itself that has played the apostate. Picking almost at random, the following is a typical utterance of Luther: " I ask that men make no reference to my name, and call themselves not Lutherans, but Christians. What is Luther? My doctrine, I am sure, is not mine, nor have I been crucified for any one. St. Paul, in I Corinthians iii, would not allow Christians to call themselves Pauline or Petrine, but Christian. How then should I, poor, foul carcase that I am, come to have men give to the children of Christ a name derived from my worthless name? No, no, my dear friends; let us abolish all party names, and call ourselves Christians after Him Whose doctrine we have."

The controversial incident of the " burning of the books " in the year 1520 illustrates Luther's attitude toward the claim of Rome to be the true Church of Christ. When an attempt was made, rather unsuccessfully, to burn Luther's writings, he responded in kind by publicly burning, not only the Canon Law and the attacks upon him by Eck and Emser, but the papal bull known as *Exsurge Domine,* which contained his formal excommunication from the Church of Rome. As he stood before the fire, Luther said, " Because thou hast brought down the truth of God, may the Lord today bring thee down unto this fire." The significance of this spectacle lies in the obvious implication that Luther's response to his own excommunication from the Church of Rome was to excommunicate both the pope and Rome from the Church of Christ. In thus repudiating Rome, Luther was demonstrating his own allegiance to the catholic Church and Rome's willful self-exclusion.

All the Reformers, including Melanchthon and Bucer as well as Luther, and Zwingli, Bullinger, Cranmer, and Knox as well as Calvin, had what amounted to a holy horror of schism from the Church of Christ. " So highly," wrote Calvin in his *Institutes,* " does the Lord esteem the communion of his Church, that he considers every one as a traitor and apostate from religion, who perversely withdraws himself from any Christian society which preserves the true ministry of the word and sacraments." It was because he felt that Rome no longer had the true ministry of word and sacrament that Calvin was so severe in his condemnation of the pope and so insistent that the Reformation was in the true succession of catholicity. In his important tract *On the Necessity of Reforming the Church,* written in 1544 and addressed to the Diet of Spires, Calvin made a prolonged and detailed response to the charge that the Reformation was basically schismatic. Concluding the essay, he said: "I deny that See to be Apostolical, wherein nought is seen but a shocking apostasy — I deny him to be the vicar of Christ, who, in furiously persecuting the Gospel, demonstrates by his conduct that he is Antichrist — I deny him to be the successor of Peter, who is doing his utmost to demolish every edifice that Peter built — and I deny him to be the head of the Church, who by his tyranny lacerates and dismembers the Church, after dissevering her from Christ, her true and only Head."

The same appeal to the apostolic consensus is found in the earliest creeds and confessions of the Reformation, virtually all of which take pains to emphasize their full acceptance of the so-called ecumenical symbols, the Apostles', the Nicene, the Chalcedonian, and the Athanasian Creeds. In the Augsburg Confession of 1530, the primary creedal authority of all Lutheran Churches, the doctrinal section concludes with the statement: "This is about the sum of doctrine among us, in which can be seen that there is nothing which is discrepant with the Scriptures, or with the Church Catholic, or even with the Roman Church, so far as that Church is known from the writings of the Fathers. This being the case, they judge us harshly who insist that we shall be regarded as heretics " (Art. XXII). The Gallican or French Confession of 1559, originally drafted by Calvin, speaking of the evils of the Roman Church, says: " Therefore we condemn the papal assemblies, as the pure Word of God is banished from them, their sacraments are corrupted, or falsified, or destroyed, and all superstitions and idolatries are in them. We hold, then, that all who take part in these acts, and commune in that Church, separate and cut themselves off from the body of Christ " (Art. XXVIII). The Second Helvetic Confession of 1566, the work of Bullinger, which had wide currency outside Switzerland among the Reformed Churches of Hungary, Poland, France, Holland, England, and Scotland, begins by quoting both the old Imperial Edict of A.D. 380, which defines heresy as any departure from the Apostles' and Nicene Creeds, and a trinitarian symbol of Pope Damasus, who so stoutly defended the orthodox faith against Arians and Apollinarians at the Council of Constantinople in A.D. 381. It then goes on to say, " Since we are all of this faith and religion, we hope to be regarded by all not as heretics but as catholics and Christians."

It is this constant harking back to the New Testament that alone entitles us to define the Reformation as a deeper plunge into the meaning of the gospel. It is this evangelical loyalty that constitutes Protestantism's true charter, and when it is stressed, there is no danger of falling prey to the insidious accusation that Protestantism is a sixteenth century by-pass. And only if this tie with the gospel can be acknowledged and strengthened can Protestantism claim to be essential Christianity. The Reformation was not something new but something old; it was the reaffirmation of the gospel — the good news of what God has done for man in Jesus Christ.

THE REFORMATION WAS NOT NEGATIVE BUT POSITIVE

Just as Protestantism has frequently thought of the Reformation as a religious movement begun in the sixteenth century in reaction to the abuses of the medieval Church, so too it has been easily self-deceived about the character of its own message. If the Reformation was in fact a deeper plunge into the meaning of the gospel, then obviously it must have been a forthright, categorical, positive proclamation of the good news. And yet from the very beginning and until the present day Protestantism has been saddled with the false inference that it is intrinsically reactionary, antagonistic, and negative.

There are clear and sufficient reasons why this impression should have become so entrenched. The very words " Reformation " and " Protestant " have negative implications and associations. If the medieval Church was torn with abuses of all kinds and stood in need of re-formation, it is natural to think of the reforming movement as set in opposition to the *status quo* and resulting in a strong protest against all that was taken to be erroneous. This, indeed, may well be one's first impression on looking into the early writings of either Luther or Calvin. What the Reformers seem most concerned about is the defection, the immorality, the unspiritual character of the Church of their own day, and they exhaust their most violent language upon all such conditions. " It is a horrible and frightful thing," wrote Luther in a characteristic passage, " that the ruler of Christendom, who boasts himself vicar of Christ and successor of St. Peter, lives in such worldly splendor that in this regard no king nor emperor can equal or approach him, and that he who claims the title of ' most holy ' and ' most spiritual ' is more worldly than the world itself. He wears a triple crown, when the greatest kings wear but a single crown; if that is like the poverty of Christ and of St. Peter, then it is a new kind of likeness." Calvin spared the Church of his day nothing. " If any one," he said, " will closely observe and strictly examine this whole form of ecclesiastical government, which exists at the present day under the Papacy, he will find it a nest of the most lawless and ferocious *banditti* in the world. Every thing in it is clearly so dissimilar and repugnant to the institution of Christ, so degenerated from the ancient regulations and usages of the Church, so at variance with nature and reason, that no greater injury can be done to Christ than by pleading his name in defence of such a disorderly government."

A first glance at the Reformation creeds and confessions of faith seems to confirm this reactionary attitude, for in stating their own beliefs Protestants appear to have been primarily interested in showing what it was that they did not believe. A notable example of this is found in the so-called Second Scots Confession of 1581, rightly termed " The Negative Confession." The document is brief and outspokenly antipapal. We quote only the condemnatory clauses of one section: " We detest and refuse the usurped authoritie of that Romane Antichrist . . . his tyranous lawes . . . his erroneous doctrine . . . his fyve bastard sacraments . . . his blasphemous opinion of transubstantiation . . . his divilish messe . . . his worldlie monarchie and wicked hierarchie . . . his erroneous and bloddie Decreets."

Fortunately this kind of creedal statement did not predominate, although far too much invective has been retained by modern Protestantism. It may be argued that polemic of this kind is salutary on certain occasions, and the Counter Reformation of the Roman Church may be regarded as having been provoked by the insistent rebukes of the Reformers. It may even have some place in contemporary Protestantism, as many would assert. Forthright Protestant apologetic, when confronted with aggressive Romanism, ought not to mince its words or refuse to take a stand. Wherever the Roman Church is in the majority and does its best to subjugate and curtail the Protestant minority, as in Spain, Mexico, Quebec, and certain countries of South America, the first principle of Protestant defense may well be a critical and negative one. In America, however, and in every country where the Protestant tradition has prevailed, there has been a steady decline of such negative invective and a studious effort on the part of modern Protestant confessions of faith to be irenic rather than polemic. But the growth of tolerance has not completely eliminated the negative approach to Protestantism. It is customary, for example, even in our own day, to define the beliefs of Protestantism *as over against* the doctrines and practices of the Roman Church. We are told by a contemporary interpreter that the " cardinal principles of Protestantism " are the right of private judgment *as over against* the Roman doctrine of the Church, justification by faith *as over against* justification by works, the supreme authority of Scripture *as over against* the infallibility of the pope, the sanctity of the common life *as over against* Roman monasticism and asceticism, and the self-verification of faith *as over against* Roman authoritarianism.

The negative side of Protestantism has surely been overdone, and in the long run has proved a disservice and an injustice. It may well be that the Reformers were too acutely conscious of their own times and therefore addressed themselves too directly to the abuses of their day. They could hardly have done otherwise. And it is surely true that the Reformation must be seen *as over against* the medieval

Church. But the big problem that Protestantism faces in our day is not the immorality and defection of the Roman Church but inner confusion as to what the Christian faith is all about, on the one hand, and laconic indifferentism nourished by our contemporary secularism, on the other. We may welcome and profit by the exposition of the Protestant faith given by one who knows the Roman Church from the inside, preferably a converted Roman Catholic, but we do not believe that *only* one who knows the Roman Church is in a position to understand Protestantism. Luther and Calvin were themselves reared within the Roman fold and they spoke to those who were Roman Catholics. But Protestantism today has generations behind it who have never known any other Christianity than the Protestant denomination in which they were born. Important and distasteful as the contemporary Roman situation may be, particularly on the question of State and Church, our chief concern is not to show how we differ from Romanists, but to indicate in clear and unmistakable terms just what it is we do believe. The way to confront the Roman problem in our day, and indeed the way in which the Reformers actually won their own following, is by showing in doctrine and life that Protestantism is true Christianity. That cannot be demonstrated by polemics or any other kind of negative strategy, and the Reformers, we can believe, would have got nowhere if this had been their sole weapon of attack.

The Reformation was a deeper plunge into the meaning of the gospel, and it was the rediscovery of the good news about God in Christ that made Protestantism in its greatest moments a living, vital, and unequivocal manifesto of divine truth. The recapture of that positive creative note is the crying need of our day. It is not only reform that we need, but a positive affirmation of faith. Indeed it may be argued that reform is not possible until there is a revival of religious conviction. It was this evangelical assurance in the Reformers that distinguished their efforts from all other reform movements, some of which were current at the time of the Reformation. We have learned that the Reformers were by no means the only ones who were disgusted and shamed by the medieval situation. In addition to Wycliffe and Hus, who are well enough known, there were others like the Carthusian monk, Dionysius, Jacob of Jüterbock, John of Wesel, Thomas Gascoigne, John Trithemius, and Matthew of Cracow. There were great preachers like Savonarola, learned scholars like Erasmus, and concerted efforts like the Conciliar Movement all of which pleaded for reform. But reform did not come within the Roman Church until after the Reformation. Luther and Calvin may have been bolder and more daring, but it was not their reform platform alone that turned the tide. It was their assurance that the gospel of the living God had been freshly disclosed to them, and it was this that gave point and power to their reforming activities. The lack of this empowering evangel was the fatal weakness of their contemporaries, which prevented them from achieving what many of the best spirits felt was so desperately needed.

If Protestantism is to speak with positive and persuasive conviction, it must do more than attack the evils of the time. It must make the plunge into the gospel that the Reformers made. Only then can it emerge a professing Protestantism and be, as a consequence, a reforming Protestantism.

THE REFORMATION WAS NOT SO MUCH A THEOLOGY AS A TESTIMONY

The deeper plunge into the gospel that the Reformation made resulted not only in a criticism of the abuses of the existing Church but in a rewriting of the theological text-books, Biblical commentaries, creeds, catechisms, and confessions of faith. The rediscovery of the gospel message demanded expression, and the Reformation made full use of all the means of communication available. Protestantism in years past has been proud of this theological articulation and has derived satisfaction from the intellectual awakening which it produced. If no one within Protestantism arose to compete with Thomas Aquinas' monumental and massive *Summa Theologica,* it was because the scholastic system, with its reliance upon the opinions of the Fathers and the Aristotelian philosophy, had been almost completely jettisoned by the Reformers in favor of a theology based upon the Word of God. From their pens flowed translations of the Bible; innumerable commentaries, tracts, and essays of all kinds; doctrinal systems like Calvin's *Institutes;* and a whole procession of creeds and articles of belief.

In the years that followed upon the Reformation, this theological activity increased rather than diminished; the doctrinal issues were more tightly drawn; disputes arose within otherwise harmonious groups; creeds began to take on a polemical and apologetic tone; and something of the medieval scholastic method was reintroduced into Protestant thought. Luther, who did not write a systematic theology, soon became for the Lutherans the champion of doctrines and distinctions with which he was not much concerned. Calvin's *Institutes* was set up as the standard of the Reformed faith, and certain controversial sections, such as election and predestination, were further developed and elaborated, as at the Synod of Dort in 1619, which defined the " five points " of Calvinism against the Arminians.

This later theological trend was not without its critics, and movements like Pietism in Germany and the Wesleyan revival in England were conscious protests against a too rigid theological structure. Moving in the opposite direction, deism and rationalism attacked the post-Reformation theology in the interests of a newly emancipated reason and paved the way for the movement of skepticism of the nineteenth century.

In our own time Protestantism is in the unhappy position of being aware on the one hand of this theological heritage, and at the same time increasingly conscious that it does not and perhaps cannot hold to the faith as expressed in this post-Reformation period. The old controversies that split the followers of Luther and Calvin do not concern us any longer. The differences among the Lutherans cited in the Formula of Concord of 1580 are studied only by historians and antiquarians. Calvin's *Institutes* has long ceased to be a text-book. The union of Presbyterians and Methodists in Canada in 1925 rang down the curtain on the Calvinistic-Arminian tangle once so divisive. The Church of England has buried its Thirty-nine Articles at the back of the Prayer Book, and Methodists by and large are not even aware of Wesley's Articles of Religion. In the meantime such Protestant groups as the Congregationalists, the Baptists, the Disciples, and others make much of the fact that they are noncreedal Churches, and now and again someone is sure to arise and call for a religion of " deeds not creeds." Apart from a few conservative fundamentalistic segments, Protestantism today is not covetous of the theological enthusiasms of the post-Reformation era. This may be an indirect cause of the plight of contemporary Protestantism and a direct cause of the widespread modern doctrinal illiteracy, but, be that as it may, the fact remains that somewhere along the line something has gone wrong.

In reacting and withdrawing from the kind of Reformation theology that has been transmitted through the seventeenth and eighteenth centuries, contemporary Protestantism has become uneasy about its loyalty to the Reformation as such. This has been brought about by a failure to distinguish between the theology and the testimony of the Reformation. We have been insisting that the Reformation was a deeper plunge into the gospel, a rediscovery of the good news of God's grace in Christ, and it is this that we have in mind when we speak of the testimony of the Reformation. The important thing to notice about the relation of Reformation theology and testimony is the sequence. The testimony comes first; the theology is the result, the by-product, the reflective response.

The Reformers did not take up their pens to write new theological treatises because they were interested in writing new books. Churchmen did not sit down together to formulate articles of faith in order to provoke a revival. It was exactly the reverse. Books poured from the Protestant presses because the new-found evangel must be publicized and let loose in the world. Creeds were written because the Church already believed something and wanted to express this faith as intelligently as possible. Luther and Calvin would have been shocked and chagrined to know that later Protestants would speak of them as founders of new theological systems. Luther never tired of repeating that his sole test and source of faith was the Word of God, and that is why there are so few complimentary allusions in his writings to the opinions of the Fathers. Calvin, to be sure, wrote what may well be called a systematic theology, but it was based upon the structure of the Apostles' Creed, and for such distinctively Calvinistic issues as predestination he appealed not only to Augustine but to Paul. The earliest Reformation creeds invariably show their allegiance to the creeds of the ancient Church and rarely define doctrine with reference to the Reformation itself.

Furthermore, it must be emphasized that the Reformation attitude toward the Word of God as the final authority for faith and life made impossible any closed system of theology. The Reformers did not write as if they had the final word, though they could be dogmatic enough. They were clear that if it is the Word of God and not the words of men that determines the faith, then any theology, no matter how Biblical or evangelical, must be at best only a faltering and stuttering effort to express the inexpressible. It is a quite typical remark of Luther's that " if one should come who knew the sense of the Word better than I, then I should close my mouth and keep still, and receive knowledge from him." When Calvin comes to discuss predestination, he says: " To desire any other knowledge of predestination than what is unfolded in the Word of God, indicates as great folly, as a wish to walk through unpassable roads, or to see in the dark. Nor let us be ashamed to be ignorant of some things relative to a subject in which there is a kind of learned ignorance." This same caution is often expressed in the Reformation creeds. For example, the relatively late Westminster Confession of 1647 apparently includes itself when it says: " All Synods or Councels since the Apostles times, whether general or particular, may erre; and many have erred. Therefore they are not to be made the rule of Faith or practice; but to be used as an help in both."

It was the great tragedy of the post-Reformation period that it forgot this initial caution about theological systems and attempted to set up rigid doctrinal structures which would not only give expression to the new-found faith but act as containers of it. Thus Protestantism moved from the fluid to the static conception of theology, faith became assent to right doctrine, the Word of God became a theory of Biblical inerrancy, and creeds were thought of as the receptacles of the faith. The sequence between testimony and theology was broken, or worse yet, the testimony itself was frozen into the molds of theological systems. The animating spirit of the Reformation was suffocated, and there was left a vertebrate but cold doctrinal skeleton.

The story of this post-Reformation decline is a long and tedious tale which should be told in more detail, but here our purpose is simply to indicate the change that took place after the first pulse beats of the Reformation and how the initial Reformation testimony was lost sight of, distorted, and obscured. It is imperative to be clear about this shift in emphasis, for it is this post-Reformation theology that has largely shaped our idea of the Reformation. We have inherited the scholastic legacy of later theologians and later creeds, which in basic ways deflect the true light of the Reformation. Our idea of what Protestantism stands for is taken from this post-Reformation theology, and, while we may not altogether lose sight of the testimony of the Reformation, we yet fail to see it as the dynamic source and norm of Reformation theology.

There is, furthermore, something presumptuous about the search for a comprehensive system of theology. There are paradoxes and mysteries in the very essence of the Christian faith that foredoom such a procedure to failure. There is the implication in such a quest that somehow man can manipulate God's truth and put it into neat, prearranged categories. That is why a static orthodoxy can easily become complacent and self-satisfied. It believes that it *has* God's Word in a system for all to see and recognize. In this sense Roman Catholicism is systematic and authoritarian in a way that Protestantism can never be. Protestant theology, if it is loyal to the Reformation testimony, must always think of itself as under the judgment of the Word of God, and for this reason always inconclusive and fallible as a system.

If we are to recapture the testimony of the Reformation, we must see that the ultimate authority of faith and life is not a system of beliefs about God but God himself. Just as the medieval theology stood in need of reformation, so too all theology at all times stands in constant need of reformation. For this reason Protestant theology can never become completed or fixed or final, and any system, no matter how excellent, is only a makeshift, a tentative, fallible thing of man's design.

All this is not meant to disparage theology or to give aid and comfort to those loose-jointed Protestants who think they can easily dispense with a vertebrate structure of belief. The Reformers did not hesitate to plunge into the deepest theological problems, but they did so only after they had first plunged into the gospel. First the testimony, then the theology. Emil Brunner thinks this sort of sequence could be maintained if Protestantism abandoned the word and idea of " dogma " altogether and spoke instead of " confession." The doctrine of the Church, he says, is a confession of what it believes; it is not itself the object of belief. Theology in itself is not necessary for salvation, but it *is* necessary. Its task is to guard against error and false doctrine, to provide a basis for catechetical instruction, and to suggest a comprehensive view of the Biblical revelation.

We hear much of the restoration and revival of theology in our time. Protestantism must welcome this and should make its contribution toward a more adequate and relevant doctrinal position. It will do this, we believe, only if it is true to the testimony of the Reformation, which, in turn, is simply the gospel of God in Christ.

What, then, we may ask, is the permanent significance of the Reformation and what attitude should contemporary Protestantism assume toward it? We have been suggesting that the abiding insight of the Reformation was the rediscovery of the gospel. It was this that animated and undergirded the life and work of the Reformers and enabled them to launch out into the modern era with a sense of divine purpose and vocation.

Historically speaking, contemporary Protestantism is bound by ties of heritage with this sixteenth century phenomenon so that it is quite impossible to understand the present situation in Protestantism without retracing the long and devious development of Churches, sects, creeds, and theologies. But is there a bond between the Reformation and the present that is more than historical? On this question there would be differences of opinion. Some Protestant Churches are self-consciously linked with the Reformation and regard it as their supreme responsibility to perpetuate in our day the gains made by the Reformation. Others would be willing to recognize the historical continuity between the sixteenth and twentieth century, but would think of their responsibility as the further development, the bringing into full flower, of the Reformation age. And between these two extremes there are many intermediate Protestant groups that are not sure what their relation may be to the Reformation.

It is not Protestantism's task to sustain or preserve intact all the externals of Reformation theology, Church structure, and social concern. Even those Protestant groups that regard themselves as " confessional " Churches, having doctrinal formularies stemming from the Reformation, are not in the first instance mere perpetuators of a sixteenth century tradition. It is not, as we have said, the theology of the Reformation that so much needs revival in our day as the testimony of the Reformation. Luther and Calvin may still have much to teach us, as modern scholarship repeatedly demonstrates, but their permanent significance does not lie with their systems but in their witness to the gospel. Protestantism is a professing or confessing faith in God's grace; it is not a profession or confessionalism in the sense of strict adherence to what has been laid down in another age. That does not mean that the older creeds and theological formulations must necessarily be abandoned. What it does mean is that Protestantism puts first things first: first the testimony, then the theology; first the evangel, then evangelicalism; first the act of confessing, then the confession.

The so-called noncreedal Protestant groups are right in seeing that they are not tied to the Reformation and that the final authority in matters of faith and life is not what Luther or Calvin or the creeds have said but the living Word of God. This is surely a correct interpretation, and one that would have commended itself to the Reformers themselves. It ought not to mean, however, as some have implied, that therefore Protestantism has no more than a historical connection with the Reformation. This is to deny the past and to impoverish the Protestant witness.

The relation between contemporary Protestantism and the Reformation is, therefore, one of tension between a reactionary and a revolutionary attitude. Protestantism should be conscious of its tradition and at the same time see that its obligation in our time is something more than the mere transmission of a static orthodoxy. Protestantism should be neither reactionary in the sense that it will ignore the ferment of contemporary existence by escaping into the seclusion of a sterile confessionalism, nor revolutionary in the sense that it will eschew, deprecate, or trifle with the living tradition of the past. If Protestantism can take seriously the

Reformation plunge into the gospel, it will conserve the vitality of its heritage, and it will feel anew the compulsion under the Word of God of reforming not only the lives of men and society but even the life and thought of its own tradition. That means that Protestantism's first loyalty is not to the Reformation, important as that may be, but to the gospel — the good news of God's redemptive purpose for man in Jesus Christ.

There is something inevitably elusive about the study of the Reformation simply because it demands a further recall to the gospel itself. The problem before us, therefore, is not solved when we interpret the Reformation as a deeper plunge into the gospel. The end of the search for the inner meaning of the Reformation is but the beginning of the quest for the essence of Protestantism. What is this gospel that the Reformation restored to its central position in the Church, in theology, and in the Christian life? And what does this gospel mean for us today? Protestantism's understanding of itself and its relation to the Reformation must be in terms of its answer to these basic questions.

The Gospel in Christianity

Historic Christianity *is first and foremost a Gospel, the proclamation to the world of Jesus Christ and Him crucified. For the primitive Church the central thing is the Cross on the Hill rather than the Sermon on the Mount, and the characteristic Church act is the Communion rather than the conference. Christian doctrine and Christian ethics may be the inevitable corollaries of the Christian Gospel; but they are corollaries. What is preached in the first instance is something that God has done for man in Christ.*

CHAPTER THREE

THUS FAR WE HAVE SEEN something of the plight of Protestantism and have examined into the nature and message of the Reformation, coming to the conclusion that the Reformation is to be interpreted as a deeper plunge into the gospel. If, therefore, the creative power of Protestantism is to be reclaimed, we must be crystal-clear as to what the gospel is and what its message for our day must be. The only way to determine this is by a reflective study of the word itself as it appears in the Scriptures of the Old and New Testaments. We shall not clear the way for the future by stating dogmatically in advance what we think the gospel ought to be or how our generation interprets it. If we would be true to the Reformation principle that Christian faith is subject to the judgment of the Word of God, then our conception of the gospel must be the result of a Biblical response. It is necessary at this point, therefore, to explore in some detail the use of the word " gospel," particularly in its New Testament context.

The English word " gospel " is a translation of the noun and verb forms of the Greek *euangelion* and *euangelizo* which, in turn, are used in the Greek rendering of the Old Testament, the Septuagint, for the Hebrew *besorah* and

The quotation on the facing page is from *The Mission and Message of Jesus,* page 301, by T. W. Manson. Copyright, 1938, by E. P. Dutton and Co. Used by permission.

basar. In tracing the use of the word " gospel " in the Bible
it is necessary to refer to the Greek and Hebrew for the
simple reason that the English translators have not been at
all consistent.

In the Old Testament, for example, the noun form is
sometimes translated into English as " good tidings," " reward " for the " tidings," " tidings," and once as " messenger." The verb forms are variously rendered as " preach,"
" publish," " show forth," " bringeth good tidings," " tell
good tidings," " preach good tidings," " proclaim glad tidings," " publish the tidings." In other words, " gospel " is not
used as a translation of the Hebrew equivalent in any Old
Testament passage in either the King James Authorized
Version of 1611 or the American Standard Version of 1901.

In the New Testament there is a great variety of English
renderings. The Greek noun form is quite consistently translated as " gospel " in the King James Version, the American
Standard Version, and the Revised Standard Version of 1946.
In two instances (Rom. 10:16 and Rev. 14:6) where the
American Standard has " glad tidings " and " good tidings,"
the Revised Standard has returned to the King James with
" gospel." But when one looks at the Greek verb forms, there
appears to be no rhyme or reason in the way the English
translators reproduced the Greek for " gospel."

Frequently in the King James Version, some form of the
verb " to preach " is used either by itself or in conjunction
with " gospel." Other alternatives are " show," " bring," " de-
clare " the " glad tidings " or the " good tidings." In the
American Standard the Greek verb forms are usually given
as " preach " or " bring " the " good tidings " with a marginal note in most instances giving the word " gospel." This
is quite inconsistent with the same version's use of the noun,
which, as we have indicated, is nearly always given as " gos-

pel," and here the marginal notes read " good tidings." In other words, the American Standard puts " good tidings " into the text for the verb, giving " gospel " as an alternative, whereas for the noun, " gospel " is in the text with " good tidings " in the margin.

The Revised Standard Version, which has a tendency to go back to the King James in this respect, everywhere translates the noun forms as " gospel," and prefers either " good news " or " gospel " in the verb forms with such additions as " preach," " bring," " tell," " receive," " proclaim."

The reason why the verb forms have presented the English translators with such obvious difficulties lies in the fact that there is no suitable word in English for " to gospel." It would only confuse matters to introduce the cognate form " to evangelize " because of the restricted connotation of this word. The Revised Standard Version has succeeded perhaps better than either the King James or the American Standard in retaining some allusion to the Greek by making use of the phrase " good news," which is, of course, a literal translation of the Greek word for " gospel."

What this brief and somewhat perplexing study in the English renderings suggests is that the use of the word " gospel " in the Bible is much more extensive and consistent than the common English translations would imply. With this in mind, we may move on to a consideration of the word in the Old and New Testaments.

THE GOSPEL IN THE OLD TESTAMENT

In the Old Testament the word " gospel " as either noun or verb occurs several times, and an examination of the passages shows that it moved from a more or less secular or profane to a definitely religious or sacred usage, both of which, it is worth noting, stress the idea of " good news."

The first and early meaning of the word is found in connection with such passages as the following: the report that David has made Solomon king (I Kings 1:42); the announcement of the birth of a son (Jer. 20:15); the rejoicing of the Philistines over the news that Saul has been slain (I Sam. 31:9; cf. I Chron. 10:9; II Sam. 1:20; cf. II Sam. 4:10).

A curious feature in all these passages is the fact that while the word has definite associations with *good* news, as has the cognate word in all Semitic languages, the passages reveal a deep and bitter irony. In I Kings 1:42, for example, the news that David has made Solomon king is by no means good news to Adonijah, who fears for his life. In the quotation from Jeremiah, the news of the prophet's birth, which caused his father to rejoice, is presented in such a way as to suggest that Jeremiah wished he had never been born. In the item regarding the death of Saul, it is the Philistines alone who find the message good news. The same is true of the combined report of the deaths of Saul and Jonathan, II Sam. 1:20, which was such bad news to David that he composed a dirge on the subject. In II Sam. 4:10, the murderers of Ish-bosheth, Saul's son, bring the report of the death to David, thinking he will regard this as good news and reward them accordingly. David, however, treats them as he treated the messenger who brought him the news of Saul's death; that is, the reward for their " good " news is death. The passage is full of strange pathos and a play upon the Hebrew word for " gospel." This sardonic note finds further expression in two additional passages. In the account of the battle of the Philistines and the Israelites at Shiloh (I Sam., ch. 4), the latter are completely routed and defeated in spite of the physical presence of the Ark of the Covenant. When Eli heard the news of the disaster, and that his two sons, Hophni and Phinehas, had been killed, he was so overcome with grief that this was the direct cause of his death. The second passage is the long and involved section in II Sam. 18:19–31, in which the Hebrew word for " gospel " occurs more frequently than in any other passage. The context has to do with the reporting of Absalom's death to David, and the repeated use of the verb and noun forms for " gospel " shows how it is sometimes good news and sometimes bad news.

What does this ironic use of the word mean? Some have suggested that the word in its early usage must be understood in a neutral sense, as simply news — whether good, bad, or indifferent. In support of this it is pointed out that the Septuagint reading of II Sam. 18:27 literally means " good good-news." But it is impossible to avoid the implication of " good " news even though it may be bad news for the person involved, and comparative philology bears this out, as well as the other passages in the Old Testament which assume a specifically religious meaning.

The irony of the Old Testament passages may, indeed, be taken as a foretaste, certainly an interesting parallel, of the New Testament use of the word, where the " good " news involves not only the message of God's deliverance and redemption in Christ, but also the fact of the cross. The emphasis upon " good " news, in other words, must not be taken in a superficial or facile way. The gospel is not a fair-weather optimism, as we shall have occasion to show.

The Old Testament passages already noted do not tell us much about the religious meaning or use of the word which it comes to assume particularly in The Psalms and Isaiah. A sort of transition passage from the secular to the sacred is found in II Kings, ch. 7. This tells of the incident of the miraculous deliverance from the siege of Samaria. The four leprous men who desert to the Syrians in hope of receiving food find that the enemy has fled, and they hasten to bring the good tidings to Elisha. It is not clear that the lepers themselves thought of this " gospel day " as in any way due to God's providential intervention, but certainly that was how the prophet, Elisha, regarded it. The point of the story is to emphasize this unexpected deliverance, which confirms and authenticates the prophet's predictions even to the minutest detail.

It is this association of good news with God's intervening hand that characterizes the second group of Old Testament passages, in which the word " gospel " first takes on a sacred and religious meaning. From The Psalms the following should be mentioned: on one occasion the psalmist repeats the good news of the goodness of God in delivering his people from their enemies (Ps. 40:9); again he looks back upon God's mighty acts in the history of Israel and forward to the future in which all opposition will be overcome (Ps. 68:11); and once more he breaks into song over the deliverance of Israel and the promise of a universal divine righteousness (Ps. 96:2; cf. I Chron. 16:23).

The psalmist's praise of God's deliverance becomes in the latter part of Isaiah the good news of the Messianic hope. There are three passages, for example, that speak of the coming of the Lord which will be welcomed and heralded by the " evangelists " (Isa. 40:9; 41:27; 52:7; cf. Nahum 1:15). Commenting on these texts, Joseph Parker, the great expository preacher of the City Temple in London at the turn of the century, says, " This is the Gospel in Isaiah; this is the evangelical dawn; this is the commission of evangelization in its earliest utterances."

What this good news will mean is set forth in two additional passages (Isa. 60:6 and 61:1). The first is a description of Zion's future splendor and restoration, in which all the nations will bring tribute from all parts of the earth. In the second passage the emphasis is upon the announcement of a coming time of spiritual liberation and redemption. These words are perhaps the most important of all in the Old Testament background of the gospel, for Jesus himself took them as his text for a sermon about his own Messianic mission (Luke 4:17 ff.).

The Old Testament understanding of the word " gospel " in its sacred and religious context may be summarized under three major emphases. First, this is " good " news. The notion of joy, latent in the root itself, becomes dominant when the word is used of God's redemptive purpose. Secondly, the good news is associated with God's deliverances in times past. The hand of God in the history of his chosen people is something to sing about. And thirdly, the good news looks forward to a time when God's redemptive purpose will be fulfilled in all its glorious consummation. It is at this point that the passages from The Psalms, and especially from Isaiah, constitute the steppingstones from the Old Testament to the New Testament, from the promise to the realization, from the Messianic hope to the Messiah, from the one who proclaims the coming of the good news to the One who is himself the incarnation of good news.

JESUS AND THE GOSPEL

Turning to the New Testament, where it may be expected that the word " gospel " receives its fullest meaning, the problem of exposition and interpretation is complicated by all sorts of technical considerations. The word becomes one of the common terms in the New Testament vocabulary, and, as is so often the case with a key word, the tracing of its meaning involves much more than an examination of passages and texts in which the word occurs. The technical side of all this has been worked over by scholars and can be found in such studies as Billerbeck's *Kommentar zum Neuen Testament*, Kittel's *Wörterbuch*, and Schniewind's two volumes on *Euangelion*. It is not necessary to rehearse what has already been done so thoroughly, but it is worth trying to separate the threads of the New Testament understanding of the gospel and, if possible, weave them into a pattern that makes plain the essential meaning and significance of this basic word.

When we look at the Synoptic Gospels for information regarding Jesus' use of the word, we find either the noun or the verb form in more than twenty instances. Of these several are what may be called editorial uses, such as Mark 1:1, 14; 16:15; Matt. 4:23; 9:35; Luke 8:1; 20:1, where the writer uses the word without suggesting that it was spoken by Jesus himself. There are, however, twelve passages in which Jesus is quoted as speaking of the gospel. Jesus, for example, is reported as beginning his ministry by proclaiming, " The time is fulfilled, and the kingdom of God is at hand; repent, and believe in the gospel " (Mark 1:15. The quotations from the New Testament are from the Revised Standard Version of 1946). He tells his disciples that " whoever loses his life for my sake and the gospel's will save it " (Mark 8:35; cf. ch. 10:29). " The gospel," we are told, " must . . . be preached to all nations " (Mark 13:10; Matt. 24:14); this is referred to again in connection with the precious ointment (Mark 14:9; Matt. 26:13); Isaiah, as has already been noted, is quoted in Jesus' first public sermon (Luke 4:18); the gospel is to be preached " to the other cities also " (Luke 4:43); it is the fulfillment of the Law and the Prophets

(Luke 16:16); the poor have the gospel preached to them (Luke 7:22; cf. Matt. 11:5).

The listing of such passages as these tells little about the nature and meaning of the gospel, and when the problem of Synoptic relationships is considered, the whole question of Jesus' use of the word seems hopelessly confused. For example, although there are twelve instances where the word is included in sayings of Jesus, these tend to cancel each other out. There is no single passage in all three Synoptic accounts of a parallel nature in which the word " gospel " occurs. Of three parallel passages in Mark, Matthew, and Luke, both Matthew and Luke omit the word (Mark 1:15; Matt. 4:17; Luke 4:14 f. Mark 8:35; Matt. 16:25; Luke 9:24. Mark 10:29; Matt. 19:29; Luke 18:29). Of the two parallel passages in Mark and Matthew where the word appears (Mark 13:10; Matt. 24:14. Mark 14:9; Matt. 26:13), Luke has no parallel for one and omits the word in the other (Luke 21:9-13). Of the passages in Luke, one is a quotation from Isaiah (ch. 4:18; cf. Isa. 61:1 f.), one has a parallel in Mark who omits the word (Luke 4:43; cf. Mark 1:38), and still another has a parallel in Matthew who omits it (Luke 16:16; cf. Matt. 11:12 f.). There is, therefore, only one passage in which Luke agrees with either Mark or Matthew in reporting a saying of Jesus that involves the word (Luke 7:22; cf. Matt. 11:5). Added to this is the complete absence of the word in the Fourth Gospel.

This has led some scholars to conclude that Jesus probably never used the word at all, while others feel that it is impossible to know with any certainty whether he did or did not. The fact that all three Synoptic Gospels, however, present Jesus as using the word deserves as much consideration as the fact that they disagree as to when and where he used it. Ultimately the question cannot be solved by textual inquiry and must be treated in the context of the disciples' faith in Jesus as the Messiah. This is Gerhard Friedrich's conclusion in his article in Kittel's *Wörterbuch.* " The question," he says, " whether Jesus used the word ' gospel ' or not is in the last analysis the question of his self-consciousness as Messiah. If he thought of himself as the Son of God, as one who would die and be raised again, then he would have thought of himself as the content of his message to his disciples. His gospel, then, is not a new doctrine; but rather he brings himself. What makes up his Person constitutes the content of the Gospel. Therefore, for his disciples, the ' gospel ' means the disclosure of the mystery of the Messiah."

The one indubitable fact amid all the perplexities of Synoptic criticism is that the word " gospel " was used by the followers of Jesus to express not only the content of his teaching but the good news of the Messiah himself. The word was used *for* Jesus by those who understood him, and his message as good news. As R. W. Dale put it in a fine epigram more than fifty years ago, " Jesus came not so much to preach a Gospel as that there might be a Gospel to preach." Those who wrote the New Testament were agreed on that. What they knew about Jesus could best be described as gospel — not simply because he brought good news, but because for them *he* was good news. There was an intimate association in their minds between the preaching and the Preacher, between the message and the Messiah, as the phrase " for my sake and the gospel's " makes clear, and four times in Acts the Greek uses the striking phrase " to gospel Jesus " (Acts 5:42; 8:35; 11:20; 17:18). Whether or not, therefore, the word " gospel " was one of the common words in Jesus' vocabulary, it was seized upon by the disciples and apostles as a term descriptive of what they conceived his mission and message to be. This would lead us to expect a wide and comprehensive use of the word in the rest of the New Testament, and this is exactly what we do find, particularly in The Acts and the Pauline Epistles.

THE APOSTOLIC GOSPEL

The first use of the word " gospel " in connection with the disciples is in the account of Jesus' mission to the Twelve, which is summed up in the words, " And they departed and went through the villages, preaching the gospel and healing everywhere " (Luke 9:6). When the apostles were imprisoned and later released, " every day in the temple and at home they did not cease teaching and preaching [the gospel of] Jesus as the Christ " (Acts 5:42). After Stephen's martyrdom, " those who were scattered went about preaching [the gospel of] the word " (Acts 8:4). Certain apostles from Cyprus and Cyrene " spoke to the Greeks also, preaching [the gospel of] the Lord Jesus " (Acts 11:20).

More specifically in connection with the preaching of the gospel many persons are mentioned: Philip (Acts 8:12, 35, 40); Peter (Acts 10:34, 35; 15:7; cf. I Peter 1:12, 25; 4:6, 17); Peter and John (Acts 8:25); Paul (Acts 20:24 and frequently in the Epistles); Paul " and his company " (Acts 13:13); Paul and Barnabas (Acts 14:7, 15, 21); Paul, Barnabas, " with many others also " (Acts 15:35); Paul and Silas (Acts 16:10); Paul, Silvanus, and Timothy (I Thess. 2:3, 4); Titus (II Cor. 8:18); Timothy (Phil. 2:22; I Thess. 3:2); Euodia, Syntyche, Clement, " and the rest " (Phil. 4:2, 3). In addition to these references, the authors of The Epistle to the Hebrews and The Revelation of John both make use of the Greek word twice (Heb. 4:2, 6; Rev. 10:7; 14:6).

The most interesting thing about the disciples' and apostles' use of the word for " gospel " is the obvious consensus among them that there is one gospel and not many. Each in his own way gives individualized expression to the gospel, but all seem united by a common conviction that the gospel itself is one. There are not, in other words, different gospels which derive their distinctiveness from the personalities or the messages of the writer. The gospel is one, and the followers of Jesus speak with one voice and with unanimity when they refer to the gospel.

Paul on several occasions speaks of " my " gospel in such a way as to suggest that it was somehow a personal affair of his own, but this is not his meaning (Rom. 2:16; 16:25; I Cor. 15:1; II Cor. 4:3; Gal. 1:11; 2:2; I Thess. 1:5; II Thess. 2:14; II Tim. 2:8; cf. II Cor. 11:4; Gal. 1:6). He uses the personal pronoun, not in order to draw attention to *his* message, but as an indication that he has made the gospel his own by appropriating it, believing it, responding to it. Paul never suggests that his gospel is in any way different from the gospel that the other apostles preached. That is why he speaks of " our " gospel which is not only an editorial pronoun but links his own preaching with that of the other disciples, and on two occasions he warns the Corinthians and the Galatians against accepting " a different gospel " (II Cor. 11:4; Gal. 1:6). In fact, he goes out of his way to vindicate his right to call himself an apostle in order to authenticate his gospel and to curtail what must have been a common criticism, namely, that his gospel *was* different because he was not one of the Twelve.

This apostolic consensus about the oneness of the gospel is given further significance by the common conviction that the gospel is something that has been given to them in trust. The New Testament writers everywhere give the impression of a sense of mission, urgency, authority, trusteeship, responsibility, and obligation. They do not think of their message as a philosophy of life that has grown out of a school of thought. The gospel is God's good news to mankind. It is not something they have suddenly hit upon and regard as a good idea; it is a divine message which, in the first instance, they have heard, and because of which they forsook all to proclaim it to others. This gives the New Testament the undertone of a compelling enthusiasm. The preaching of the gospel is undertaken by men who feel the force of a divine commission.

The apostles are not like high-minded and noble volunteers who agree to pioneer with a new idea. They are laid hold upon by a sense of obligation and urgency which they understood as coming from their Master himself. When Jesus sent out the Twelve to preach the gospel, they may have had some misgivings about their assignment. But after the resurrection, when he had been restored to their midst and the whole meaning of his life and death had become clear to them, they thought of their task of proclaiming the gospel as a divinely committed trust which must be discharged.

The apostle Paul, who had less reason than Jesus' own disciples to feel the force of this divine imperative, was nevertheless particularly anxious to make plain that he too was an apostle in the same sense as they. He goes out of his way to emphasize this, and in doing so gives added confirmation of the idea that apostleship is a being-sent-out to preach the gospel. The first sentence of his greatest epistle begins, " Paul, a servant of Jesus Christ, called to be an apostle, set apart for the gospel of God " (Rom. 1:1).

THE NATURE AND CONTENT OF THE GOSPEL

The use of the word " gospel " in the New Testament indicates not only the oneness of the gospel message and the divine imperative to make it known but also the content of the message, what it is all about, its substance and its meaning. If all the relevant passages are studied and correlated, a definite pattern gradually takes shape. The content of the gospel is not, of course, a rigid, inflexible thing, but certain major accents recur with such frequency and unanimity as to suggest a more or less definite framework which gives the gospel its form and substance. This can be expressed in a series of three spiral or cumulative propositions.

Jesus Christ is at the heart and center of the gospel. There can be no doubt about this. The gospel is a Christocentric message. It is not a philosophy, or a theology, or a system of ethics. It is Jesus Christ. This is not merely an inference from the whole tone and temper of the New Testament; it is the obvious implication of the use of the word " gospel " itself. Such phrases as the following are characteristic: " The beginning of the gospel of Jesus Christ "; " They did not cease teaching and preaching [the gospel of] Jesus as the Christ "; " Preached good news about the kingdom of God and the name of Jesus Christ "; " Told him the good news of Jesus "; " Preaching good news of peace by Jesus Christ (he is Lord of all) "; " Preaching [the gospel of] the Lord Jesus "; " Preached [the gospel of] Jesus and the resurrection "; " The gospel of his Son "; " The gospel of Christ "; " The promise in Christ Jesus through the gospel "; " Preach [the gospel] to the Gentiles the unsearchable riches of Christ "; " The gospel of our Lord Jesus."

If this Christocentric emphasis is examined further, it is revealing to see what kind of reference is made to Jesus Christ. One clue is to be found in the name itself — Jesus Christ, or Jesus as the Christ. The gospel is the good news that the Old Testament prophecies regarding the coming Messiah have been fulfilled in Jesus. This man of Nazareth *is* the Christ. He is the incarnation of God's promise of de-

liverance. The teacher, the miracle worker, the teller of
parables, the despised and rejected rabbi — *he* is what God
has been saying in times past. The gospel is the good news
that Jesus is the Christ.

This means, further, that the gospel is a personal message.
It is not merely a doctrine or a way of life; it is the good
news about a person. That is why the New Testament is
concerned to record and preserve the facts and incidents in
the life of Jesus. He was born of the seed of David, of Mary
the wife of Joseph; he ate, slept, prayed, wept, was thirsty
and tired; he suffered, was killed, and was buried. These
biographical details are not only literary trimmings; they
remind us that the gospel has to do with a living, historical
person.

But the gospel, it must be added, is not the good news
about a man. It is not the teaching or the personality of
Jesus that constitutes the gospel. To speak of a man as the
Christ is blasphemy or idolatry. What determines the New
Testament reference to Jesus Christ is his unique relation-
ship to God. This man is the Christ because he is the Son of
God. The incarnation is not the good news that the son of
Mary became the Son of God, but that the Son of God be-
came the son of Mary. This leads to the second proposition
about the content of the gospel.

*Christ is at the heart and center of the gospel because God
was in Christ.* The New Testament nowhere gives the impression that what Jesus said was important because he said
it or because of its intrinsic truth, but because it was as if
God himself had said it. The divine guarantee that God was
in Christ is what gives the gospel its distinctive authority
and power. The writers of the Gospels are not concerned to
elaborate on the earthly life of Jesus as though this was of
itself important, or for the sake of filling in local color to

enhance the historical person. The historical events are important because it is through them that God reveals himself. Thus the historical Jesus is never himself a subject of interest or concern in the New Testament. The historical life of Jesus is not the gospel. The life of Jesus only becomes gospel by the recognition of the fact that God was in Christ. That is why there are repeated references in the New Testament not only to the gospel of Christ but to the gospel of God (Mark 1:14; Rom. 1:1; 15:16; II Cor. 11:7; I Thess. 2:2, 8, 9; I Tim. 1:11; I Peter 4:17), and the explicit reminder that the gospel is of God, not of men (II Cor. 4:4; Gal. 1:11; I Thess. 2:4). This is borne out by many such phrases as " Good news about the kingdom of God "; " The gospel of the grace of God "; " The gospel . . . the power of God "; " An eternal gospel."

Whether it is more nearly correct, therefore, to begin the definition of the gospel with Jesus Christ or with God in Christ, it is not easy to say. The two emphases are so closely related that they are really one. It is Christ who makes the gospel visible, tangible, personal; but it is God in Christ that makes the gospel authoritative, effective, compelling.

All this means that the gospel is the revelation of God in history. The gospel is the good news of what God has done. It is a news report, a proclamation of historical events, a chronicle of dates, figures, places, and persons. But it is not just the history or the events that make up the gospel. It is the fact that there is a meaning and a fulfillment of history in one event, in one person. Christ is not only the best or highest revelation of the nature and purpose of God; he is God himself in the flesh. He is what God has revealed himself to be in history and event; he is what God has to say to us.

It was the resurrection of Christ that put the divine

guarantee on the gospel as the good news of God in Christ. This was *the* new event in the divine revelation, and it became the cornerstone of the New Testament faith. It was not only a miracle; it was an event: a dead man was raised from the dead and restored to his friends. It was not only a revelation that God was in Christ; it was good news: evil, sin, and death have been conquered. This was the visible manifestation of the eternal in time: the prophecy of the past and the hope of the future have become a present reality; the hereafter is here.

It was this conviction that God was in Christ — not only in his life (incarnation) and his death (atonement), but in his resurrection — that gives the New Testament its boundless enthusiasm and its contagious sense of joy, victory, and triumph. The gospel of God in Christ is the good news that a new age has dawned, that in Christ the darkness has passed, that the new man in Christ is a new creation. This leads to a third proposition regarding the content of the gospel.

Christ is at the heart and center of the gospel because God was in Christ for man's redemption. The gospel includes the life of Jesus, but it is not biography; it involves the teaching of Jesus, but it is not doctrine or ethic; it is a revelation of God, but not objective truth; it is the divine intervention into history, but not merely a manifestation of God's sovereignty. The New Testament gospel is redemptive, soteriological. It is concerned not only with the revelation of God in Christ, but with the revelation of God in Christ as Redeemer and Saviour. It is only when the redemptive note is sounded that the gospel becomes good news. It is not necessarily good news to know that God was in Christ unless we also know that this was for us. The gospel does not stop with the proclamation of what God has done in

Christ; it is the good news that he has come for our redemption.

The purpose of the New Testament is not only to preserve the record of divine revelation but to elicit man's response. It is only through response in faith that the gospel becomes good news for us. The gospel, therefore, is not only truth but salvation, not only doctrine but new life, not only revelation but response, not only proclamation but power. That is why the New Testament is as much concerned to tell what the gospel does for a believer and means to him personally as it is to tell what the gospel is. Hence we find the gospel linked with salvation (Rom. 1:16; I Cor. 15:2; Eph. 1:13; II Thess. 2:14); conduct (II Cor. 9:13; Gal. 2:14; Phil. 1:27); faith (Acts 15:7; II Cor. 9:13; Col. 1:23; Heb. 4:2); peace (Eph. 2:17; 6:15); new life (Acts 14:15; I Cor. 4:15; II Thess. 2:14; II Tim. 1:10; I Peter 1:23–25); hope (Col. 1:23; II Thess. 1:7, 8); joy (Luke 2:10; Acts 8:8); the Kingdom (Mark 1:14, 15; Matt. 4:23; Luke 8:1; Acts 8:12); power (Rom. 1:16; II Tim. 1:8); light (II Cor. 4:4); truth (Gal. 2:5, 14; Col. 1:5).

Response in faith to what God has done in Christ for man's redemption results not only in new life for the individual believer but in a new common life. It is through the community of believers, the fellowship of the Church, that the gospel is made known, preached, and spread abroad. It was to the Jewish community, the people of the covenant, that the gospel first came, and it was the fulfillment and consummation of that divine election and separation. " Jesus as the Christ " means not only the fulfillment of Old Testament prophecies about the Messiah but also the fulfillment of the Old Testament covenant. Jesus taught and preached in the Jewish Temple and synagogues, he gathered twelve around him as disciples, and after his resurrec-

tion the company of believers were quickly but imperceptibly drawn together in their common faith and allegiance.
The missionary message of the gospel resulted in similar
groups and communities all over the civilized world, and
it was out of the Christian fellowship that the New Testament itself was written down and preserved.

This fellowship in the gospel is not a voluntary association of like-minded people who band together for conveni-
ence or expediency; it is the " body of Christ," the visible expression of the incarnation. The gospel is the good news
which the fellowship shares and celebrates, for example, in
the Lord's Supper. And it is the fellowship that demonstrates
the relevancy and significance of the good news in the world.

The gospel is the good news of God in Christ for man's
redemption. This is the core and essence of the Christian
faith. Whatever else may be said about Christianity, this at
least must be said. Whether we like it or not, whether we
approve of it or reject it, whatever our response may be,
Christianity stands or falls on the gospel. It is the source of
all true theology, the impulse of Christian ethics, the theme
of preaching, the charter of evangelism, the bond of fellowship. It was the gospel that sustained martyrs, inspired reformers, and called forth missionaries. It is the gospel that
judges us and not we the gospel. It is the gospel that warns
the Church to be the Church and challenges Christianity in
every age to be true to its divine source. It was the gospel that
the Reformers rediscovered in the sixteenth century, and it
is the gospel that Protestantism today must recapture if it
is to stand upon its feet and proclaim the living Word of
God.

The New Preaching of the Gospel

M uch of our preaching *in Church at the present day would not have been recognized by the early Christians* as kerygma. . . . *The verb " to preach " in the New Testament frequently has for its object " the Gospel." Indeed, the connection of ideas is so close that* keryssein *by itself can be used as a virtual equivalent for* evangelizesthai, *" to evangelize," or " to preach the Gospel." It would not be too much to say that wherever " preaching " is spoken of, it always carries with it the implications of " good tidings " proclaimed.*

CHAPTER FOUR

WHAT WOULD IT MEAN for Protestantism to confront its own present confused situation with a fresh vision of the gospel? It is not possible to explore all the ramifications of such a provocative question, but there are two large areas in which the Protestant witness would undoubtedly be strengthened and deepened, and we may concentrate on these. In this chapter we will examine the effect that a serious concern for the gospel would have upon the whole matter of preaching or proclaiming the Christian message. In the next chapter we will inquire into the significance of the renewed interest in our day in evangelism, and we will try to relate the gospel to this pressing and basic problem.

THE PROCLAMATION OF THE GOSPEL

Phillips Brooks's classic definition of preaching as " the bringing of truth through personality " may be interpreted in any one of three different ways. Brooks himself regarded it as comprising two basic elements, namely, the truth or the message that is to be preached, and the person or personality of the preacher. But the process of bringing the truth *through* personality, the problem of communication, is itself a necessary aspect of preaching, involving all the arts and

The quotation on the facing page is from *The Apostolic Preaching and Its Developments,* page 5, by C. H. Dodd. Copyright, 1937, by Harper & Brothers. Used by permission.

artifices of what is called homiletics. All these elements are obviously interrelated and dependent upon each other. If the preacher has nothing to say, no amount of eloquence or personal enthusiasm will achieve the purpose of preaching. If he has a message, but does not succeed in putting it across, as we say, the preacher fails just as miserably. And if the message and the technique of delivery are not gathered up into that intangible thing we call personality, so that preaching and preacher become blended together, there will be no personal commitment, no personal conviction, and no personal response.

Important and necessary as the other elements of preaching may be, it is with only one of these three emphases that we wish chiefly to be concerned here, namely, the truth — or the message, as we have called it. This is surely the place to begin in any discussion of preaching, although by itself it is an incomplete description unless the other two elements are kept in mind. It seems justifiable to restrict ourselves to this aspect of preaching, moreover, for the simple reason that it is on this point rather than on the other two that there is manifest confusion.

Protestantism has always put a strong accent on preaching. The pulpit is in many ways the distinguishing symbol of Protestantism, whether it be literally in the center of the church or not. Sometimes this is taken to be a weakness of Protestantism or an overemphasis. We have heard the plea for a moratorium on preaching, and we are experiencing the rise of a liturgical protocol which seeks to put the pulpit in its proper place. But Protestantism began with preaching, as has every great religious movement, and it has been strongest and most influential when the centrality of preaching was taken for granted.

Why is this? Why all the talk, the advice, the exhortation,

the enticement, the cajolery? Why the oratory, the eloquence, the fireworks, the silver tongue? Why should the preacher, who is as often as not a very ordinary human being, presume to stand before a group of people and speak to them? Why is it that with few exceptions Protestantism, unlike Roman Catholicism and Greek Orthodoxy, makes so much of preaching? It is just because there is uncertainty and ambiguity at this point that there is a real need to rethink the whole matter of the relation of preaching and Protestantism.

Preaching stems from the conviction that there is something important and worth-while that needs to be said and must be said. That " something " is the gospel — the good news of God in Christ. The gospel is a story, a narrative, an epic tale of what has happened. The event of which the gospel tells is good news, glad tidings of great joy, the voice of liberation, and the trumpet blast of victory. It is good news because God has come in Jesus Christ for man's redemption. It is this fact, this happening, this divine revelation that constitutes the truth and the message of Christian preaching. The gospel is a story to tell, good news to proclaim, divine truth to communicate. The preacher, as P. T. Forsyth liked to put it, stands, not in the tradition of the Greek orator, but in the direct line of the Hebrew prophet. He is a man of God, not primarily because of his own spiritual or personal qualifications, but because a message, a word of God, a " burden " has been placed upon him. What he has to say is not important because *he* says it, or because of the way in which he says it, but because God has spoken in an act of cosmic significance.

Preaching, in the context of the gospel, assumes consequently larger proportions than is commonly recognized. Preaching is not restricted to the sermon and the pulpit.

Preaching is the proclamation of the gospel — whether by homily, in worship and sacrament, through education, or by means of Christian living and social witness. The way in which the gospel is made known is the task and problem of evangelism, and we are coming to see that we have not yet begun to exhaust the possibilities of communication. But regardless of *how* the gospel is to be preached, it is the *what* of the gospel that is our immediate concern.

There is, of course, nothing really "new" about this interpretation of the meaning of preaching. It has been said before in every generation, and countless books and lectures have been addressed to ministers reminding them that the gospel is the subject and the object of their preaching. What is new, however, is the rediscovery of the content and character of the gospel message, which has come to us largely from the labors of Biblical scholars, and the widening vistas and new horizons that this has opened up for contemporary preaching.

Biblical studies in recent years have made it possible to speak of preaching the gospel with a new sense of meaning and significance. The older controversy between the religion *of* Jesus and the religion *about* Jesus, which Harnack understood to result in what he called a "double Gospel," has given way to an almost unanimous conviction among Biblical interpreters of all shades of opinion that the New Testament is a basically harmonious and unified proclamation of the gospel. Differences in emphasis are surely there, but more significant than the varieties of expression is the underlying unity. It is the recognition of this unity and the exposition of its content that distinguishes contemporary Biblical criticism from that of another generation.

"Preaching the gospel" in the New Testament means proclaiming the good news of God in Christ. It is this gospel proclamation that unites the New Testament despite all variations of accent and provides the key that unlocks the mysteries and the treasures of the Biblical record.

The implication of this unified interpretation of the New Testament for the problem of preaching is tremendous and incalculable. It does not, of course, solve at one stroke all the tangled problems of New Testament criticism, but it makes irrelevant and pointless the older uncertainty about the New Testament and offers a basic consensus which gives new meaning and vitality to the gospel message. "Preaching the gospel" is now seen to be a phrase that covers the whole range of Christian testimony. It can no longer be monopolized by self-styled "evangelists." It has nothing to do with a particular kind of oratory or the emotional appeal associated with revivalism and sensationalism. It is not preaching that is "orthodox" according to the theological standards of a traditional "evangelicalism." It is not preaching "the blood," or the "rugged cross," or the Virgin birth, or the inerrancy of the Bible. Nor, to take the other side, is it the preaching of the words of Jesus, the "simple" gospel of the Nazarene. It is not the Sermon on the Mount, the Golden Rule, the Fatherhood of God and the brotherhood of man. It is not democracy, or the New Deal, or socialism, or civil rights, or progressive education.

RESTORING THE LOST RADIANCE

The New Testament consensus regarding the preaching of the gospel may be illustrated as a sort of two-beat rhythm accenting, first, the good news proclaimed and, second, the fact of God in Christ for man's redemption. What is preached is taken to be good news because of what it is. The redemptive revelation of God's grace *is* good news. The overtones of joy and victory that everywhere pervade the

New Testament are not the artificial good cheer of a determined effort to keep smiling. The exhilaration and ecstasy of the New Testament are not the result of a Pollyanna or sky-blue utopianism but the inevitable response to the story of divine redemptive love. "Preaching the gospel" means the communication of this good news about God in Christ. It is not a sermon, but it is the source of all true preaching. It is not a doctrine, but it is the basis of all sound theology. It is not an idea or a point of view, but it is the structure of Christian philosophy. It is not a way of life, but it is the animating dynamic of the Christian ethic.

All this is so basic, so self-evident, and yet so foreign to contemporary ideas about preaching, that it is worth examining further this two-beat rhythm of the New Testament note. If, then, we would be true to the New Testament accent, we will preach *good news*. There will be an element of joy, victory, triumph, and gladness in our preaching. At the "Faith and Order" assembly during the Lausanne Conference in 1927, Timothy Tingfang Lew pointed out that the word for "gospel" is reproduced in Chinese by two words meaning "happiness from on high." That is an excellent translation and expresses exactly the New Testament mood. In the Early Church Clement said that the Holy Spirit is a "glad Spirit." Augustine prayed, "My God, my Holy Joy." Francis of Assisi was as much concerned to live a life of gospel gladness as to follow the vow of poverty. Charles Wesley sang:

> "In the heavenly Lamb
> Thrice happy I am,
> And the heart it doth dance at the
> sound of His name."

It is no accident that Christianity is the most joyful singing religion in the world. There are some faiths that rob life of its joy and seek to dampen the human spirit, but not the Christian faith.

Now it is clear that this note of joy has largely disappeared from our preaching. It seems to be incongruous with the sober and solemn times in which we live. There is so much to lament, so much misery, such widespread anxiety, that any emphasis on joy and gladness seems out of place and unrealistic. And yet the New Testament, which is realistic enough, is shot through and through with good cheer. The Christian above all others should give expression to this holy gladness, but he too has been caught up in the pervasive gloom that characterizes our contemporary mood. There is an uncertainty and dejection about the Christian witness that is the very antithesis of the New Testament. And frequently the reason for this morose frame of mind is a very curious one indeed. The Christian Church is here to proclaim the glad tidings of salvation; but it is downcast and dispirited even though it has discovered that this is actually what the world most needs to hear!

Karl Barth, in a speech read over the British Broadcasting Corporation a few years ago, said that if he were a politician or an editor of a newspaper he would ask the Churches of the land the following questions: "Why are you not saying what you ought to say, and saying it with power and eloquence? Why don't you force us to pay attention to you and listen to you? We should like to see you less timid, more consistent, bolder. We often have the impression that you are afraid — of what really? And you spread so little light and joy around you. When you make yourselves heard, it is usually with cares and complaints, lamentations and accusations." That is something to think about. We have inverted the gospel of " good tidings of great joy," the note of gladness has soured, and the buoyancy, vivacity, and rejoicing have gone out of our witness.

Something of the joy of the Christian faith, to be sure, is felt at Christmas and at Easter, but, for the most part, preaching today is more concerned with the crisis of our age, the problems of social life, and the tensions of personal existence. These issues can certainly be made the subject of preaching, but what the preacher has to say about them ought to be in terms of the good news of God's grace. This need not degenerate into the pronouncing of pious platitudes about Jesus as the solution of all our problems. It can be as realistic as a labor union or a psychiatrist's couch, but if it springs from the gospel, the element of joy must be apparent. The lost radiance of the Christian faith must be restored, so we can say with the psalmist, " They looked unto him, and were radiant " (Ps. 34:5). It is just here that the esoteric sects of our time, like the Jehovah's Witnesses, can teach the established denominations a lesson in maintaining the spiritual glow. Their enthusiasm may be emotionally surcharged and artificially manipulated, but they know what is meant by the joy of salvation.

Unless the gladsome note can once more become the dominant theme of gospel preaching, not only will the rift between the New Testament and present-day Christianity widen, but it is hard to see what possible or useful function preaching can serve in our day. The preacher can hardly hope to compete with the news analyst, the statesman, the dramatist, the novelist, or the psychiatrist. All are better qualified to speak of this world's ills and none lacks an attentive audience. Unless the preacher can proclaim the good news of " happiness from on high," it is an open question whether he has anything at all worth saying that cannot be said better by someone else.

WHAT MAKES THE GOSPEL GOOD NEWS

The gospel note of gladness is what it is because of the second rhythm beat of the New Testament emphasis. We can preach glad tidings only if the subject of our preaching is God's grace in Christ. That is the good news we preach. What we have to say *is* good news. The proclamation of the divine redemptive revelation is what accounts for the New Testament joy. Something has happened! God has done something! Have you heard the good news? This is the occasion and the source of the Christian exultation.

What happened? What has God done? What content does the New Testament put into the preaching of the gospel? Biblical scholarship in recent years has helped us to answer these questions by focusing attention upon the actual reported sermons and addresses of the early apostles which the New Testament retains for us. Professor C. H. Dodd, of Cambridge, and others who have followed his lead have distilled out of the New Testament, particularly in The Acts and the Pauline Epistles, what appears to be the earliest apostolic preaching. Without trying to reproduce in any detail what has already been done many times, we may note simply that this apostolic preaching of the gospel is made up of five basic emphases.

The first point in the apostolic preaching of the New Testament is the announcement that the Old Testament prophecies regarding the coming Messiah have been fulfilled in Jesus Christ. That is to say, the apostles began back in the Old Testament. They asserted that the next and final chapter in the long story of God's redemptive plan for Israel is the story of Jesus Christ. The new age to which the Old Testament looks so longingly, and at times so wistfully, has actually come to pass and now exists (cf. Acts 2:16; 3:13; 10:36; 13:17; Rom. 1:1-3).

This first point is followed by explicit reference to the earthly historical life of Jesus. This is presented in the apostolic preaching, not merely as biography or exhortation to "follow the leader," but in terms of the incarnation, God becoming flesh, the eternal in time. Sometimes this is suggested very briefly as "born of the seed of David," a historical clue, so to speak, like the reference in the Creed, "suffered under Pontius Pilate" (cf. Acts 2:22, 23; 3:13; 10:38, 39).

The third accent of the apostolic preaching falls upon the death of Christ, the cross, atonement, and reconciliation. The gospel does not stop short with the life or teaching of Jesus. It includes the cross, and, indeed, this receives more explicit mention than the life or the teaching. But the death of Christ is not an isolated fact and derives its full meaning only in view of the incarnation that precedes it and the resurrection that follows (cf. Acts 2:23; 3:13, 14; 4:10; 5:30; 10:39; 13:27-29; Gal. 1:3, 4; 3:1; I Cor. 15:3, 4).

Of a piece with the incarnation and the atonement is the resurrection, the fourth major apostolic emphasis. It is the resurrection that sounds the note of joy in what might otherwise be a tragedy. It is by virtue of the resurrection that Christ is exalted as Lord of the new age which his coming has already inaugurated (cf. Acts 2:24, 32, 33, 36; 3:15; 4:10, 11; 5:31; 10:39; Gal. 4:6; I Thess. 1:10; I Cor. 15:1-8; Rom. 1:4; 8:34).

The final point in the apostolic preaching is the call to repentance. The proclamation of the gospel is the recitation of certain facts or events, but it closes with a summons to believe, to repent, to be baptized, to appropriate the gift of God's redemptive revelation in Christ (cf. Acts 2:38; 3:19; 4:12; 5:31; 10:43; 13:38, 39; Rom. 10:8, 9).

Having set forth these five points, however, we must hasten to say that such a description of apostolic preaching does not do justice to the element of variety which the New Testament itself suggests. We must not imagine that the preaching is stereotyped or rigid in this way, but rather that there is an underlying unity even when there are wide variations in expression. There are differences, for example, in the Pauline and Petrine preaching, just as there are differences in the four Gospels. But the message proclaimed, wherever it is found in the New Testament, is essentially the same.

The most immediate reaction to this brief review of the apostolic preaching is the felt difference between New Testament and contemporary ideas of what preaching is all about. Not only has the note of joy and gladness gone out of our witness, but we do not seem to be preaching about the same thing. And that perhaps is why there is so little good news in present-day preaching. What makes the New Testament conception of preaching so strange and alien to our modern ways of thinking is the fact that " preaching the gospel " in the New Testament is a restricted and definitely circumscribed idea. The apostolic preaching is all alike. Apart from minor variations, the central theme is always the same. The message is limited, the same divine events are repeated over and over again with a kind of steady monotony. There is no branching out into the bypaths of culture and life, no discussion of current political theory or economic problems, no allusions to literature or philosophy or what other people are thinking about. The apostolic preaching reiterates the same points, tells the old, old story in what would today be regarded as a tedious monotone.

Put over against this New Testament self-limitation such a description of contemporary American preaching as Alec R. Vidler, the editor of the Anglican journal *Theology,* ventured after a recent visit to this country. Taking care to qualify his estimate, he nevertheless felt strongly about the preaching that he heard. " What shocks me most of all," he said, " is the character of the preaching that seems to prevail in your churches. . . . So far as I can ascertain, the paradigm of American preaching is: ' Let me suggest that you try to be good.' Moralistic homilies are still the order of the day. . . . Preachers take texts from Scripture (though they do not always do that much), and treat them as mottoes or captions under which they excogitate some religious or moral lessons that have little, if any, direct relation to the Scripture they have quoted. . . . Your preachers, it seems to me, are still advocating justification by good works of one kind or another (they may be very orthodox or very ' Catholic ' good works); they are not proclaiming the Gospel of salvation by faith in Jesus Christ " (*Theology*, February, 1948).

Whether this visitor from England rightly assessed the character of the American pulpit is perhaps an open question. It is interesting to observe, however, that shortly after the publication of his reflections a similar criticism appeared (in *Christianity and Crisis*, April 12, 1948) by Bernard W. Anderson, an instructor in religion at Colgate University. Faced with the question, " What shall I preach ? " the modern minister, so we are told, responds in many different ways. He may have the " gift of gab " which, in a sense, releases him from the challenge of the question altogether. Or he may gather a number of striking illustrations and anecdotes and do his best to tie them together like a bunch of spring flowers. He may turn hopefully to the numerous homiletical " helps " which suggest sermon topics for every Sunday of the year prepared by some expert who has explored a new " mine " of material and garnered preaching " values " from current literature. He may follow the

" Church year " or the yearbook of his own denomination and preach on Mother's Day, Thanksgiving, and pensions for retired ministers.

Happily this is more of a caricature than a portrait, but with the stringency and rigidity of the apostolic preaching in mind it serves to illustrate how far it is possible to diverge from what the New Testament understands by preaching. One thing is clear: the New Testament variety is much more difficult. It is harder to repeat the same subject day in and day out, year after year, and still make it compelling and appealing. It is much easier to find a new subject for each sermon and to pick one's themes from the whole range of contemporary culture and literature. To preach the gospel with full relevancy and with imagination and insight is the most exacting task a preacher can undertake, and perhaps the reason why real " expository " preaching is so rare these days is simply because it is such hard work. And perhaps it is also true that the present-day preacher is as distracted as he is because his preaching is so diffused and scattered. The problem of " holding " a congregation's attention and enthusiasm may actually be accentuated by this frantic search for new topics and catchy texts. For, whether he likes it or not, the contemporary preacher *is* restricted. He is no longer the symbol of education, culture, and learning in his community as he once was. The radio, television, and the press bring more entertainment, more current events, more oratory and eloquence than the modern preacher can hope to emulate.

The self-limitation of the gospel message, however, does not mean that preaching must be uninteresting, irrelevant, or dull. It is at this point that Phillips Brooks's emphasis on the personality of the preacher is so important. The gospel message when preached with vigor and pertinent application has never been considered banal or flat. The musician must keep within the limits of his medium, the painter is restricted to his canvas and his brush, the novelist must work within the limits of his vocabulary, but music and painting and literature have a way of being renewed by every master artist. The gospel is not dull, but all too often the preacher is. The message is restricted but not restricting. If the gospel is at the center, the preaching can roam as far as the preacher's imagination. Preaching is the bringing of truth through personality. The gospel message is the truth; it is for the preacher to see that he does not palter with the truth.

WHERE THE GOSPEL NEEDS TO BE HEARD

To move from the abstract to the particular, from generalities to concrete examples, what would it mean for contemporary preaching if the gospel note of good news could be sounded again with conviction and assurance? It would call for a determined effort to stress what we have called the two-beat rhythm of the apostolic preaching — the element of joy and the fact that God has come in Christ for man's redemption. It would mean the recasting of what we take preaching to be. It would demand a revision of our thinking on some of the pivotal points of the Christian faith. By way of suggestion and illustration we may look briefly at the effect that the renewed preaching of the gospel would have upon our ideas of authority, God, man, and death.

The gospel note on the question of authority is the good news that God has spoken. We are living in an age when the question of authority is of primary significance, and it is a question that the preacher knows is addressed in a peculiar way to him. What is his authority for what he has to say? How can he dare to stand on his feet and open his mouth? What authority does he have and to what authority does his preaching appeal? The gospel is the preacher's authority — God has spoken, God has acted, God has come! The preacher is not called upon to vindicate his own personal authority in the sense that what he has to say depends upon his education, his insight, his wisdom, or his imagination. He is called upon to preach the gospel, which is God's living word to men. He cannot do that, of course, without education, insight, wisdom, and imagination. And he must be able to say with the apostle, " *my* gospel." But the preacher's own personality and faith are not the authority by which he speaks. The preacher is a prophet, one who speaks for God, and like the prophets he does not draw attention to himself or ask that his own ideas be taken seriously. He has been entrusted with a message from God, and it is this that constitutes the authority of preaching. This does not mean that the preacher must become an irrational dogmatist. But it does mean that he must be clear as to where his authority for speaking lies.

The recapture of this gospel note of authority would be the greatest good news for preacher and people alike. No longer would the Church need to hang its head when asked by the world, " What do you have to say? " No longer would the preacher feel the intolerable burden of trying to justify himself and his literary creations in the sight of his people. The gospel is God's truth, and God is not mocked.

The gospel note regarding our conception of God is the good news that God is like Jesus Christ. The preacher must talk about God. But, as Barth has reminded us, there is certainly something absurdly presumptuous about this. How can a mere man talk about God? Can the creature describe his Creator? Well, we have done our best. We have proved the existence of God. We have seen God in nature, in history, in conscience. We have predicated God's attributes, ex-

plored his decrees, and probed into his will. We have even
defined him. A contemporary American philosopher of religion suggests that " God is that kind of interaction between
things which generates and magnifies personality and all its
highest values."

This may be interesting, but it has nothing whatever to
do with the gospel. The gospel is the good news that God
has revealed *himself*. If we leave Christ out of our definition
of God, we can never hope to understand the New Testament. The Apostles' Creed has perhaps unwittingly en-
couraged us to think that first we can affirm our belief in
God Almighty and then move on to Jesus Christ. The
Apostolic Benediction is nearer the gospel sequence, " The
grace of the Lord Jesus Christ, and the love of God . . ."
We do not first know something about God and then something about Christ. Luther complained that the theology of
his day described Christ in terms of God rather than God
in terms of Christ. But that implies that we could first
know something about God apart from Christ and then use
our knowledge to describe Christ. We must, the Reformer
demanded, learn to recognize God in Christ.

What this would mean for our modern interpretation of
God as well as of Christ can only be described as a revolution. And that it would instill the gospel note of joy and gladness into our preaching is beyond doubt. The Christian dares
to be presumptuous in talking about God, and he does so
with all the awe and wonder of the New Testament because God has made himself known in the flesh.

*The gospel note regarding man is the good news that in
Christ there is a new creation.* It is imperative that we have
right ideas these days about man. What is man? Is he a
child of nature, a servant of the state, a discontented animal
— a " chimera," as Pascal would say? The traditional theo-

logical approach to this question has been through the doctrine of sin. Man is a sinner who has fallen from grace and stands in need of redemption. In recent years it has become the theological fashion to speak of the revival of the doctrine of sin. Current events seem to give point and meaning to the dogma as never before and lift it out of the doctrinaire discussions of another age. The " crisis theology " is supposed to have rediscovered man's depravity, and Kierkegaard, C. S. Lewis, and Reinhold Niebuhr are quoted to confirm the trend.

All this may be to the good. The New Testament does not slur over man's sin. The cross of Christ, one of the points of apostolic preaching, implies atonement for sin. But the gospel note is not sin but grace, not depravity but redemption, not misery but joy. The Apostles' Creed does not contain a clause, " I believe . . . the sin of man." It is implied, no doubt, but what it affirms is " the *forgiveness* of sins." The specific gospel emphasis about man is that in Christ, to use the Pauline figure, there is " a new creation." Redemption is the death of the " old Adam " and the new birth in Christ.

What we need today in our preaching is not less talk about sin but more assurance of salvation. Sin is not something that in our day needs to be demonstrated, and unless the preacher can say something more than that man is a sinner, he will not have anything very distinctive to say at all. What he can say, and what others are not saying, is that man can be reborn. That is good news and a gospel worthy of the name. Henry van Dyke was once asked what hymns he would exclude from the hymnal, and he responded, " All those that speak of hell; hell is nothing to sing about! " And sin is nothing to sing about. The New Testament rarely speaks of sin without also speaking of the forgiveness of sin, and the hymnbook is there to remind us that down through the ages it has been forgiveness that has caused Christians to burst into song.

The gospel note regarding death is the good news that Christ is the resurrection and the life. The modern mood questions whether there is any good news at all about death. Isn't it the final humiliation, the equal fate of good and evil, the ultimate seal of failure? We avoid this pessimism as best we can either with the help of the undertaker's art or by mouthing unconvincing platitudes about the immortality of the human spirit. But the problem of death is not so easily solved, and since we must all die, this is a truly perennial and ever-present question.

It is surely an indictment of modern preaching that it has so little to say on this subject. Search the homiletical magazines through, and rarely will you come across a sermon on life beyond death. Easter, to be sure, provokes the subject, but most of our thinking about immortality is more Platonic than Biblical. We talk about the natural immortality of the soul; the New Testament speaks of the miraculous resurrection of the body. Is this a crudity, a remnant of primitive psychology, an accommodation to an unscientific way of thinking? And if so, must we say the same for the resurrection of Christ?

Just as the New Testament links together sin and grace, so it sees death as over against life. In Christ, so Paul tells us, we are dead to sin and raised to newness of life. We are crucified with Christ, yet Christ lives in us. We are buried with Christ, yet Christ is our life. There is a dialectical character to the gospel eschatology which transcends our usual distinctions between death and immortality, the here and the hereafter, time and eternity. The death of which the New Testament speaks is not merely the moment of physical death, nor is life the same as immortality. To be in Christ is to be dead now and to be resurrected now. The Fourth Gospel speaks of this as " eternal life." It is not merely the extension of life beyond death; it is a new kind of life which begins when Christ lives in us, and because he lives we shall live, or, better still, we *do* live. " This is eternal life, that they know thee the only true God, and Jesus Christ whom thou hast sent " (John 17:3).

The new preaching of the gospel turns out to be the old preaching of the gospel. And that is what we might expect. It is not something new that is needed in contemporary preaching but something old preached in a new way. What we have tried to suggest for such basic issues as authority, God, man, and death could be extended to include all the problems and questions of life and thought. What, for example, is the gospel note regarding history, the relation between faith and conduct, society and civilization? We have yet to see an adequate and comprehensive evangelical ethic that would take full cognizance of the New Testament preaching and the perplexities and confusions of contemporary existence.

It must not be assumed, however, that by emphasizing the gospel note of joy, gladness, triumph, and victory, an easy optimism is meant. The gospel is not a fair-weather message. The Christian faith is not, as it has been charged, an escape from reality, a flight of fancy, an opiate for the people. Sometimes that is what it is taken to be, but that is a perversion of the gospel, a counterfeit that is easily recognized. " Preaching the gospel " is not blinding our eyes to life's depressing realities. The gospel is not something to save us from the tragic sense of life; it does not make light of pain or sorrow or suffering. It is a message of courage and hope and good news *in the midst of* evil, darkness, sin, and death. The authentic gospel note is found in such New Testament outcries as: " Count it all joy, my brethren, when you meet various trials "; " Who shall separate us from the love of Christ? Shall tribulation, or distress, or persecution, or famine, or nakedness, or peril, or sword? . . . No, in all these things we are more than conquerors "; " In the world you have tribulation; but be of good cheer, I have overcome the world."

The Evangelistic Perspective

As we have studied evangelism *in its ecumenical setting we have been burdened by a sense of urgency. We have recaptured something of the spirit of the apostolic age, when the believers " went everywhere preaching the word." If the Gospel really is a matter of life and death, it seems intolerable that any human being now in the world should live out his life without ever having the chance to hear and receive it.*

It is not within the power of man alone to create a new evangelistic movement. But the Holy Spirit is at work in men with men. In the past He has from time to time quickened the Church with power from on high. It is our earnest hope and prayer that He will do a mighty work in our day, giving the Church again wisdom and power rightly to proclaim the good news of Jesus Christ to men.

CHAPTER FIVE

E VANGELISM IS CONCERNED with the Evangel, the good news of God in Christ for man's redemption. It is the presentation and communication of the gospel to all mankind. It is significant, therefore, that " evangelism " is staging a comeback and is once again in good and respectable standing in the religious vocabulary. The restoration and revival of the word, with all that it implies, is one of the more hopeful signs of contemporary Protestantism.

The history of evangelism is the history of the Christian Church. From its beginnings in apostolic times down through the centuries the good news of the gospel has been carried from generation to generation and from continent to continent. At certain periods there has been more geographical extension of the Christian faith than at others, and at times certain individuals arose who became the pioneers of a crusading evangelism which swept whole areas and populations into the Christian fold. Running parallel with this history is the great modern missionary enterprise which penetrated into faraway lands and planted the seed of the gospel among the non-Christian peoples of the world. So magnificent is this history in terms of personal daring, sacrifice, and testimony, that it can be said with assurance that whenever evangelism has been vigorous, the life of the Church has been strong and radiant. When we look back upon the history of the Church, evangelism — whether at home or abroad — has been like a sensitive thermometer registering the warmth and the health of the Christian faith.

At the present time we seem once more to be poised on the threshold of a great evangelistic period of Christian history. Evidence of this is found in the aroused attitude of the traditional Churches which fear for their existence and the continuance of the Christian witness as the onslaughts of secularism and religious indifferentism make their inroads upon the Church. The Church of England, for example, which has had such a molding influence upon the British character, has become alarmed over the statistics that less than ten per cent of the population have any vital Church affiliation. On the continent of Europe, particularly in Germany, the birthplace of the Reformation, the Church situation has become radically disrupted by the Nazi regime and the aftermath of the war. In America, where the statistics of Church membership are encouraging, practically every large Protestant denomination is engaged in a program of evangelism, and Churchmen are not willing to equate numerical strength with vital Christianity. We have not yet moved into the new period of evangelism, but the Church is expectant with a sense of urgency.

THE EXPANDING DIMENSIONS OF EVANGELISM

It is the element of crisis in contemporary Christianity that raises anew the whole question of evangelism — its nature, its purpose, its methods, and its message. There is little enthusiasm for restoring the older forms of evangelism, and a certain suspicion attaches to the methods of what is known as revivalism. The evangelism of our day, so we are being told on all sides, must be something more than emotionalism and sensationalism, fiery oratory and catchy tunes, mass meetings and circus tents. And the reason for this quest for an altogether new approach is due to the fact that we are living in a revolutionary age which presents for the Christian faith problems never before encountered on such a vast scale. This is as it should be. Evangelism must be in touch with the temper of the times if it is to be realistic, and its methods must change with the times if it is to be effective.

The changes that have taken place in recent years, which lie behind the reawakened sense of the cruciality and urgency of evangelism, may be set down in a series of propositions: (1) The task of evangelism until very recent times has been generally regarded as the special vocation of selected individuals or groups, while today it is commonly agreed that evangelism is the prime responsibility of all who call themselves Christian and of all Churches that profess the gospel. (2) Evangelism is now seen to be, not merely *one* of the ways in which the Church witnesses to the gospel, but *the* way and the *only* way. There is something incongruous about the minister who now and then preaches an evangelistic sermon or finds an occasion to " put on " an evangelistic campaign. There is something wrong about the organization of committees of evangelism — whether in denominational headquarters or in councils of Churches. Evangelism is not one of many jobs that the Church has to do but the only one that can possibly justify any other interests it may have. (3) The recognition of this responsibility has been rightly conceived as the major concern of the ecumenical movement. Evangelism is the business of all the Churches in their program of co-operation and union and in their efforts to meet with a united front the peculiar problems of our day. (4)

One of these problems that particularly affects the Church is the growing realization that this is a post-Christian or un-Christian age. The Churches of the West, once so strong and confident, are now aware of the fact that in many ways they have not made so great an impression upon society as they thought. Church membership in many lands has dwindled and the voice of the Church is not heeded as it once was. Evangelism, therefore, becomes in this situation a matter of existential importance. (5) This means that the older distinction between a pastoral ministry and a prophetic ministry must be abandoned. There can be only one ministry — evangelism. The Church is not divided between settled communities strong in the faith which need only a pastoral oversight and the unchurched and heathen to whom a prophetic missionary approach is needed. (6) As Kierkegaard has shown us, the Church in a so-called Christian society may be in special need of evangelism because "the greater number of people in Christendom only imagine themselves to be Christians." This, incidentally, is why Karl Barth feels it necessary to re-examine the whole conception of baptism, for if everyone is baptized, both sacrament and Christian faith may easily become perfunctory. (7) This means that the first step in evangelism is not the "outreach" of the Church but the inward conversion of the Church itself to the gospel.

This widening and at the same time constricting evangelistic perspective has laid special problems upon the Church of our day. For example, it is now seen that evangelism in terms of social witness is not enough. The Christian character and the Christian ethic do not perpetuate themselves apart from the Christian faith and the Christian gospel. In the Early Church what is known as *didache,* or moral teaching and instruction, largely took the place of *kerygma,* or preaching the gospel of God in Christ. But this was possible because the gospel was taken for granted and the ethic was the inevitable by-product of the Evangel. In our day, too, *didache* predominates, but we cannot assume that the modern understanding of the Christian ethic is the result of a serious concern for the Christian Evangel. We should like, if we could, to have the ethic without the Evangel. But the ethic by itself does not evangelize. A Unitarian spokesman says that modern ministers in his own denomination attract large audiences but do not gather congregations. A Congregationalist writer, interested in the revitalizing of the liberal tradition, confesses that the denominations that have been most advanced in social teaching have made the smallest gains in new members. Evangel without ethic is certainly sterile and motionless; but ethic without Evangel is powerless to save.

Another special problem of our time, created by the post-Christian character of society, is the growing suspicion on the part of many that somehow the Church as it now exists is in fact an obstacle to evangelism. When the Christian Commando Campaigns, an evangelistic movement begun in Britain during the war, asked its listeners for their questions, very common queries were: " What is your motive in coming to us? " " Is this a stunt to fill your empty churches? " " Have the bosses sent you? " " Why have you suddenly become conscious of the workers? " " Aren't there as good Christians outside the Churches as inside? " These questions give evidence that among many, particularly of the laboring group, there is a deep prejudice that the organized Churches somehow represent special and privileged interests that are either inimical or indifferent to the common workingman. Evangelism under such circumstances is at a tremendous disadvantage, to say the least.

With these problems in mind, it is clear that a whole new strategy of evangelism as well as a new conception of evangelism is desperately needed. Moving from the center outward, the Church must first think of itself as standing under the judgment of the gospel; then the strayed sheep — what Cyprian in the Early Church called the "lapsed"; then the secular and un-Christian within our post-Christian society; and finally the non-Christian, whom we used to call the heathen. Toward this world-wide evangelism all the mediums of modern civilization must be utilized. Radio, press, literature, drama, the movies, television — all must be put under captivity to the gospel. Social witness must not be abandoned but enlarged, for the whole of man's life must become the concern of a renewed and enlivened evangelism. A great many experiments directly pointed at the contemporary situation have already appeared, and show by their variety and influence that the Christian Church is awake to its evangelistic imperative. But strategy obviously is not enough unless we are sure what it is that constitutes the aim and goal of evangelism. Where can we look for light?

THE BIBLICAL FOUNDATION OF EVANGELISM

One of the most interesting and illuminating approaches to the whole question of what it means to communicate the gospel is to be found in a number of recent inquiries into the catechetical methods of the early Christian community. Professor Oscar Cullmann, of Basel, has reminded us of the message of the earliest Christian confessions of faith in his important essay, *The Earliest Christian Confessions* (Lutterworth Press, 1949). Philip Carrington, the archbishop of Quebec, has attempted to reconstruct the apostolic catechetical method in his book *The Primitive Christian Catechism* (Cambridge University Press, 1940). Of particular signifi-

cance for evangelism is Godfrey E. Phillips' *The Transmission of the Faith* (Lutterworth Press, 1946) for the reason
that it is written by a missionary who knows at first hand
how the problem of communication requires special consideration in connection with the non-Christian. It is the con-
tention of this latter book, and one that we may linger over
briefly, that evangelism is essentially a *transmission* of the
gospel from one person to another, from one group to another, from one age to another, from one race to another,
and from one creed to another. It is the passing on and
handing over, not only of the ideas and ideals of the gospel,
but the divine historical events of which the gospel is the
good news. It is the remembrance of things past, the calling
to mind what God has done, the didactic indoctrination of
the Biblical revelation. This is the primary intention of
evangelism, not just because the present must be understood
as emerging out of the past, or because the road to tomorrow leads through yesterday, or because we today must try
to imitate in life and thought an ancient classic tradition.
The reason for recalling the divine history of God in Christ
is that we may come to know how God acts in us and in
our world by learning what as a matter of fact he has done.

The means that such a recall must utilize in the interests
of transmission are chiefly three: the Biblical record itself,
with special reference to its narrative character; worship and
ritual; and ethical norms of behavior — both individual and
social. Through the telling of Biblical stories, and in particular the story of Jesus Christ, the divine redemptive history is
transmitted without the danger of conscious or unconscious
embellishment, rationalization, or modification. Through
worship, which includes prayer, song, sacrament, ritual, and
the reading and preaching of the Word of God, not only is
praise given but the events of divine history are brought to

mind. Through the development and promulgation of ethical standards of life, which take a distinctive attitude toward such matters as marriage, sex, treatment of enemies, and the sick and the helpless, the relation between what God has done and what we in consequence are to do is shown forth in practical experience and example. These are the ways in which the earliest Christian converts were actually instructed in the new faith — these were, and always have been, the most effective means of evangelism.

If we examine the Bible itself as containing evidences and samples of evangelistic strategy, it is surprising how much of the record can be interpreted as the crystallized instruction given to children and converts. The memory of God's creation, his election and covenant, his deliverance of Israel from the Egyptian bondage, his providence and guidance through the wilderness, his ethical commandments, and his promise of the coming " day of the Lord " — all these and more were gathered together to form the core of Jewish religious instruction. It was the prophet's function to remind the people of what God had done and now requires; it was the priest's responsibility through ritual and ceremony to bring the divine history to mind in symbolic form; it was the " wise man's " prerogative to prepare meditative and reflective epigrams; and it was the parents' continuing task to raise their children in the knowledge of this divine story so that it would not be forgotten and could be handed down from generation to generation. And to aid in this task of parental instruction all sorts of memory helps were devised — acrostics, rhythmic repetition, poetic structures, as well as the more common but no less stylized narrative forms — all of which are evident in the Old Testament writings.

When we turn to the New Testament, we discover that the Old Testament mediums for religious instruction are continued, as we should expect. Much of the material seems to group itself around the three emphases of indoctrination in the divine history (which now includes the facts of the life, death, and resurrection of Christ), worship (with the accent on the sacrament of the Lord's Supper), and ethical norms (which derive from the teaching and example of Christ). That is to say, the method of communicating the Evangel remains the same, but the content of the message has become radically transformed by the fact of Christ. Evangelism in the New Testament is no longer merely instruction in the history and meaning of God's election, but the good news of God in Christ.

If we look first to the epistles of the New Testament, where is recorded the earliest informal advice given by the apostles to the newly converted disciples, we are impressed by the conscious and repeated allusion to the "tradition" (*paradosis*) which has been handed down and which must be safeguarded and handed on. For example, Paul says, "I delivered to you as of first importance what I also received" (I Cor. 15:3), and he goes on to enumerate the salient events in connection with the life, death, and resurrection of Jesus as though this were a recognized summary of Christian instruction, as indeed it came to be in the Apostles' Creed. In the same way, speaking of the Lord's Supper, he says, "I received from the Lord what I also delivered to you" (I Cor. 11:23), and here follows the narrative description of Jesus with his disciples breaking bread and drinking the cup. Once more Paul exhorts his readers that "as you learned from us how you ought to live and to please God, just as you are doing, you do so more and more" (I Thess. 4:1), a typical remark recalling the ethical requirements of the new life in Christ. That which the apostle has "received" and "learned," the facts of the life, death, resurrection of Christ, the supreme act of Christian worship, and the new norms for ethical living, all these are in trust, so to speak, and constitute the content of the religious instruction that was given to the Christians of the Apostolic Church.

We have already seen how the apostolic preaching included the affirmation that the Old Testament promises have been fulfilled in Christ, and therefore the instruction handed on to the Christian converts, who were of course in the first instance Jews, did not abrogate or nullify the Old Testament. But the distinctive feature of the New Testament instruction is the difference which Christ makes. "You did not so learn Christ!" says Paul in warning the Ephesians against the immorality of the Gentiles (Eph. 4:20). It was because of this constant reference to Christ that the Gospels came into being. They supplied the necessary historical background material, and there seem to be suggestions, as the school of form criticism maintains, that this was done in terms of certain "forms" by which the main events in the life of Christ were transmitted from person to person and committed to memory. The teaching of Jesus, for example, in the Gospel of Matthew is set down with obvious parallels to the Old Testament. The author links certain sayings with the Prophets, the Sermon on the Mount corresponds with the giving of the Law on Mount Sinai, and there are stylistic rhythms and poetic stresses which intimate that the gospel was meant to be learned and passed on to succeeding generations.

Perhaps the clearest evidence of a corpus of received tradition is the listing of various virtues and vices which occurs so frequently in the epistles. The following catalogue is the sort of ethical code which could be easily committed to memory and transmitted from person to person, parents to children, disciples to converts — "immorality, impurity, licentiousness, idolatry, sorcery, enmity, strife, jealousy, anger, selfishness, dissension, party spirit, envy, drunkenness, carousing, and the like. . . . But the fruit of the Spirit is love, joy, peace, patience, kindness, goodness, faithfulness, gentleness, self-control . . ." (Gal. 5:19-23).

What we learn from the Bible regarding the aim and goal of evangelism is that both the Old and New Testaments are concerned to transmit the great events of divine history. The New Testament takes an evangelistic attitude toward the worship of the faithful, the education of the young, the instruction of converts, the appeal to the indifferent, and the mission to the pagan and the heathen. It is an evangelistic attitude because it is based upon the Evangel. Communicating the Evangel is indoctrination in the good news of what God has done for man in Christ.

The word "indoctrination," however, is not one that is likely to enhance the relevance of this Biblical evangelism for our contemporary situation. The word and the ideas with which it is associated are repugnant to the modern mind and seem to smack of the dictatorial kind of dogmatism and propaganda that in the political and ideological arena we have been so ready to decry. Furthermore, the sacrosanct attitude toward a received tradition sounds very much like a doctrinal or static orthodoxy to which we have no wish to return. If evangelism must be interpreted as the mechanical transmitting of accepted dogma, which in turn is memorized and repeated parrot fashion from generation to generation, surely there can be nothing here for our present-day evangelistic strategy.

This interpretation is, of course, not what the Bible means, and it is not what it has to say to us in our present distress. In fact, the Bible makes it clear that a mere traditionalism, no matter how studied and well learned, is not enough. The

Gospels are abundantly clear that the Jews in Jesus' day knew their historical facts well enough and had learned their lessons, so to speak, and yet did not really know the meaning of the revelation that had been given to them. Jesus warned the Pharisees against their own well-mastered tradition. " You have a fine way," he said, " of rejecting the commandment of God, in order to keep your tradition " (Mark 7:9). He was constantly rebuking his own disciples for their blindness, not their ignorance. He accused the scribes and the Pharisees of hypocrisy, not stupidity. The facts about Jesus' life, death, and resurrection make up a New Testament consensus which keeps within narrow confines, yet there are four Gospels, not one. Paul discusses the gospel with its meaning and implications in such a way as to suggest that it is something definite and circumscribed, but there are several Pauline Epistles and no two are alike.

The gospel is not a static thing, a doctrine to be put into a mold, a series of dates and events, a formal liturgy, or a code of ethical commandments. The gospel is the good news of God in Christ. But it cannot be preached or communicated without doctrine, historical reference, worship, or ethical implication. In other words, the Evangel is unchanging and changeless, but evangelism changes with the times and the circumstances. There is no hope for us in a mere traditionalism. Some Churches are proud of their catechetical instruction and their theological orthodoxy, but they frequently give no more evidence of the power of the gospel than those Churches that have dispensed with what they would regard as an outmoded pedagogy. But neither is there hope for us in an evangelism that cuts loose from the Evangel. Our post-Christian age does not need a different gospel or another gospel. It is not something different that we need to communicate, but something that we need to communicate in a different way. Present-day evangelism does not need a new goal toward which to strive, but a new inspiration and incentive for seeking the goal that has always been there.

A CHARTER FOR EVANGELISM

The word that best describes the evangelistic problem of the present is " perspective." Just as a landscape painter must contrive to group together on his canvas the relative positions, sizes, and distances of the objects he wishes to portray, so too the evangelistic problem is one of grouping together the contemporary world situation, the strategy and mediums for communicating the gospel, and the essential nature and content of the message to be transmitted. As in painting, so too in evangelism, the important requirement is a point of viewing to determine what needs to be foreshortened, what needs to be magnified, and how the several parts can be related to each other.

What would the outlines of an evangelistic perspective look like? What evangelistic point of viewing would give meaning and purpose to all our ideals and hopes for a more vital and extended Christian witness? Taking into account the peculiar problems that beset us, and recognizing the tension between a changeless Evangel and a changing evangelism, what basic affirmations can we make as the point of departure for an evangelistic perspective? Three, at least, can be ventured.

1. *Evangelism is a divine imperative.* Evangelism is not an optional or voluntary occupation in which a few interested persons engage. It is a mandate for all laid down by Christ himself. " Go into all the world and preach the gospel to the whole creation " (Mark 16:15). If, textually speaking, there may be some doubt whether Jesus ever uttered these

words as recorded in Mark, there is no doubt that this was the way in which the earliest disciples looked upon their discipleship. They wrote their Gospels, converted the Jews, went out to the Gentiles, because they were under a divine ultimatum. It was not merely that they heard Jesus, or thought they heard him, on one occasion tell them to go forth. All that he was and said and did for them constituted the evangelistic imperative. To preach the gospel to all creatures was not one thing among many that he said; it was the divine summons to make known all that he said.

The New Testament takes this divine decree for granted. It never argues about evangelism, as to whether it is a good thing to do or even why it should be undertaken at all. Paul speaks of his apostleship and his mission to the Gentiles as if he had no choice in the matter. " Paul, a servant of Jesus Christ, called to be an apostle, set apart for the gospel of God . . ." (Rom. 1:1). He is not a volunteer; he is a conscript. He does not choose to preach the gospel because he thinks it is a good thing to do; he is a steward of the mysteries of God.

The New Testament incentive for evangelism must be the motivation for all our schemes and plans. It is the needed corrective for much loose talk about evangelism in terms of its functional values. It is a good thing, no doubt, to spread the spirit of enlightened humanitarianism around the world. It is a noble thing to feel with Albert Schweitzer that the dominance of the white man and the exploiting civilization of our day require an expression of practical reparation for wrongs committed. It is a legitimate hope that if the gospel can be preached to all creatures the prospects of a common humanity and consequently of a common peace can be secured. It is a worthy ideal of the ecumenical movement to demonstrate the oneness of the Church by emphasizing the world mission of the Church. But let it never be forgotten that the reason for evangelism is our Lord's commandment, and not any ulterior values that it may achieve. The purpose of evangelism is not political, economic, social, or even ecclesiastical. The gospel is good news, and a divine requirement is laid upon us to spread the news. If we answer that summons and make the gospel known in all its potency and relevancy, we may be sure that it will have social and political reverberations throughout the world.

2. *Evangelism implies a basic reversal of values.* Evangelism is not the perpetuating of the *status quo*. To evangelize does not mean to plant Western Christendom in Eastern soil. When the Christian believer witnesses to the gospel, it is not *his* faith that he offers for imitation. The world mission of the Church is not the spread of cultural principles. To take the gospel to the heathen, whether at home or abroad, is not to appeal to the best that all men know or to enhance their best with Christian insights. Evangelism requires a rightabout-face, a revolution in life and thought, an upsetting of inherited values and acquired characteristics.

The New Testament speaks with one voice that the gospel changes things around in a radical way. It speaks of repentance, rebirth, redemption. It speaks of a *new* commandment, a *new* creature, a *new* man, a *new* and living way, a *new* heaven and a *new* earth, a *new* name, a *new* song — it is, indeed, a *new* Testament. " If any one is in Christ, he is a new creation; the old has passed away, behold, the new has come " (II Cor. 5:17).

The apostles use a striking illustration to give expression to this gospel transfiguration. It is drawn from the death and resurrection of Christ symbolized in the sacrament of baptism (cf. Eph. 4:17 to 6:20; Col. 3:1 to 4:5; I Peter;

James 1:1 to 4:10; etc.). The passages are worth careful study, for they all speak of " the new man " or the new birth in Christ. The suggestion is that the disciple dies to his old self by casting aside his old associations just as he would lay aside an old garment, and, as a matter of fact, as the early convert did lay aside his clothes in preparation for baptism. This is dying with Christ, being crucified and buried with him. After baptism the new man arises out of the water, a symbol of Christ's resurrection, and he is clothed with new garments. He is raised with Christ; he is a new creation; he now " puts on " the new life in Christ.

We shall make a grievous mistake if we take all this as merely symbolic and figurative. The new life in Christ *is* a new life. It is the transformation that finds expression in the discovery that " it is no longer I who live, but Christ who lives in me " (Gal. 2:20). It is the reversal of values.

Kierkegaard was right in thinking that it is more difficult to be a Christian in a modern so-called Christian civilization than in the early years of the apostolic community. Our temptation is to think that the New Testament transvaluation has been made, and to be a Christian, therefore, is to accommodate oneself to the Christian society in which one happens to live. But what if the society is not really Christian? " When all are Christians, Christianity *eo ipso* does not exist! "

The big obstacle toward evangelism is not only that we are confused about what the gospel is and how we are to communicate it to others, but that we show so little evidence of what the gospel has done to us. To say that there is not much difference between the outward appearance of a Christian and a non-Christian in so-called Christian countries is not so much a compliment to the non-Christian as an indictment of the Christian. The New Testament definition of the Christian is one who has died and been raised from the dead. He is a new man in Christ.

The reason why evangelistic appeals are ofteh met with such resistance even by those who call themselves Christians is that we do not want to be shaken out of our accepted ways of thinking and acting. And the reason why evangelism falters is because there are so few evangelists who know what it means to be buried and raised with Christ. To live " in Christ " is to live under the challenge and judgment of him who said, " Behold, I make all things new."

3. *Evangelism is between time and eternity.* We are not so confident today about evangelism as the generation of young people who banded together under the rallying cry, " The evangelization of the world in this generation." Perhaps we are too timid. John R. Mott, who began his long and distinguished career under that banner, thinks that the slogan has been misunderstood. It does not mean the converting of everyone to Christianity in one generation, but making it possible for everyone to hear and respond to the gospel. It does not mean that it *can* be done but that it *ought* to be done. Well, it was not done, it has not been done, and the question arises, Can it ever be done? How much can we expect from evangelism? Have we a right to anticipate a world-wide Christianity that would be something more than the extension of Western culture? How does evangelism fit into our interpretation of history? Does history have a meaning, a goal, a *telos* toward which we are moving? Is the evangelization of the world an event that will sometime take place in history or at the end of history? Or is that only a wistful hope, an ideal, a far-off divine event? Must we look to the Second Coming of Christ, the end and finis of history before the kingdoms of this world become " the kingdom of our Lord and of his Christ "?

It is interesting to observe that the New Testament passion for evangelism ran side by side with the eschatological hope of Christ's imminent return. The remarkable thing is that the New Testament does not regard these as contradictory or mutually exclusive. "This gospel of the kingdom will be preached throughout the whole world, as a testimony to all nations; and then the end will come" (Matt. 24:14). The eschatological hope was perhaps the reason for the urgency of the apostolic evangelism, but when the apocalyptic elements of that hope subsided and when it became clear that Christ would not return in the first generation, the evangelism continued.

This is a parable of the perennial tension between time and eternity that is so confusing for those who want a simple answer to the issues of the Christian faith in terms either of this world or of the next. But the New Testament tells us that we live between the times. God the eternal has come into time in Jesus Christ. The Kingdom is here, but it awaits its consummation. We are raised with Christ, but we look toward the last day. We must preach the gospel to all nations, but Christ will return to fulfill what he has begun. There is no easy solution to this apparent contradiction, and we shall do well to take it as it is and try to see what the dialectic of time and eternity can teach us.

So far as evangelism is concerned, we may state the tension in two propositions. One says that what we can accomplish by way of evangelism is all to the good, but we must not be too optimistic or sanguine about bringing in the Kingdom. The other proposition is that the full revelation of God's purpose will not be achieved except in an eschatological sense, but this must not lead us to despair of our present efforts. What has been accomplished by evangelism is no mean thing, as Professor Latourette's volumes on *A History of the Expansion of Christianity* have amply demonstrated. Indeed, it may be possible to speak of the present moment as "advance through storm." The Christian faith is more widely distributed throughout the world than ever before, and the "influence of Jesus" has penetrated every area of life. The evangelistic success of the Apostolic Church can be measured by the fact that a few individuals within a short time spread the gospel far and wide and outthought, outlived, and outdied the pagan world, as T. R. Glover put it. The missionary activity of the eighteenth and nineteenth centuries achieved much and prepared the way for a larger evangelism. There are today numerous examples of suggestive evangelistic approaches, such as the Iona Community in Scotland, the Sigtuna movement in Sweden, the Bossey Institute in Switzerland, and many others, which encourage us to believe that we have not exhausted the possibilities of evangelism.

But the divine imperative of Christ has not been fulfilled, and there is no prospect of an evangelistic program that will sweep all before it. It would be a mistake to put all our confidence in some one plan or in all conceivable plans. We live between the times, and the fulfillment of God's redemptive purpose is eschatological.

This does not mean that we should abandon evangelism and sit tight, so to speak, waiting silently and passively for the return of Christ. The eschatological hope does not mean the curtailment of historical existence and activity. It means just the reverse. It means that the hope of the consummation and fulfillment of God's redemptive purpose is the safeguard against despair. It means that no historical catastrophe is the end of history in the sense of finis, and that there are ever new possibilities for evangelism opening up before us. The bridegroom may delay his coming, but we are admonished to watch and pray and be alert.

Perspective is an essential requirement for evangelism, but it is not itself evangelism. A point of viewing is necessary as a point of departure, but evangelism is the rough-and-tumble work of spreading the gospel. It is possible to talk about evangelism so much that one neglects to evangelize. John Oman, of Cambridge, once gave this good advice to young ministers: " Be careful," he said, " or you will spend more time arranging your books than in reading them, and in referring to your engagements than in keeping them, and you will develop a trot that does not cover half as much ground as an easy swing, and a babble of words that does not say half as much as one quiet phrase."

The New Testament, as we have said, is not very self-conscious about its evangelism. It does not talk about it much or discuss it at length. And it may be a mark of weakness that there is so much talk about evangelism today and so little evangelism. The bishop of Worcester had this in mind when he said, " What worries me is that people form committees to teach others how to evangelize, and in many cases they have no intention of engaging in evangelistic work themselves." It would be a mistake to look too hopefully at the World Council, for example, for new leadership on evangelism, as if through some sort of ecclesiastical bureaucracy people outside the Church can be induced to become Christians. We can hardly expect others to respond to the gospel if we do not show first that we have ourselves been evangelized. Nor is it enough for the rank and file of Christians to delegate this task to selected and qualified evangelists.

It is at this point that Protestantism can make its own distinctive contribution to the task of evangelism. The Protestant doctrine of the priesthood of all believers is not only an ecclesiastical principle but an evangelistic responsibility and opportunity. Rightly understood, it could become the dynamic motivation of the rising tide of " lay " Christianity and release a latent reservoir of evangelistic witness. Properly interpreted, it would narrow the gap between clergy and laity which so often hampers and frustrates the work of the Church. Given the right emphasis, it would indicate more clearly and forcibly than doctrine and exhortation that there is no graduated hierarchy of privilege and responsibility so far as evangelism is concerned. One reason why this basic but neglected doctrine has not received its proper recognition is that it is so often understood as tending in the direction of Protestant individualism. It is interpreted to mean that everyone is his own priest. There is truth in this, of course, but what needs to be emphasized is that the doctrine was associated in the minds of the Reformers with the Church, and not with individual freedom or independence. Thus, it would be more accurate to call it the doctrine of the *common* priesthood of believers, for the Reformers meant, not merely that each man is his own priest, but that each is his neighbor's priest; we are all priests within the fellowship of Christ's Church, with the responsibilities as well as the prerogatives of the priest.

From the Protestant point of view, therefore, we are all in this business of evangelism together. There are no exceptions to the divine imperative. We need not all go out to the uttermost parts of the world, but we are to spread the gospel by word and act and example wherever we are. Such a common commitment would be the surest way to revive the glory and the power of Protestantism.

The Tomorrow of Protestantism

As in all Christianity *from the beginning, continuing and growing vitality depends upon the degree to which Protestantism is a channel of the eternal Gospel. Protestantism came into being chiefly because through its great spirits the Gospel found fresh outlet. The revivals which have marked the course of Protestantism have sprung primarily from the same source. Other factors, some political, some economic, some personal, have been partly accountable. The most powerful and the one without which the others would have been impotent is the Gospel. In a continuing and growing loyalty to the Gospel in understanding and in full and joyous commitment is the hope of Protestantism. If Protestantism embodies the Gospel it will go on and grow. If it loses it or becomes too stereotyped to give it free expression it will dwindle and the eternal life in the Gospel will break out elsewhere and create for itself fresh channels.*

CHAPTER SIX

THE THESIS THAT UNDERLIES the studies we have made is that Protestantism is an interpretation of the gospel — the good news of God in Christ. In so far as Protestantism gives expression to that gospel, it is not only positive but Christian. The rediscovery and recapture of the gospel was the abiding and permanent contribution of the Reformation, from which historically and spiritually Protestantism in all its diverse forms may be said to find its dynamic source. This does not mean that the gospel was completely hidden during the long period from the close of the apostolic period to the sixteenth century. The Middle Ages from the Protestant point of view were the " dark ages," but it was not a complete blackout of the gospel. In personal piety, in worship and liturgy, in devoted Christian lives, the gospel was manifestly present and at work. That is why it was possible for Luther to appeal to what the common people dimly but surely felt. The Reformation, in this sense, was not a revolution, but a rediscovery of what had been obscured. The rediscovery of the gospel in the sixteenth century, as the Reformers repeatedly maintained, was not something new but something old.

Nor does the recapture of the gospel made at the time of

The quotation on the facing page is from *The Christian Outlook*, page 158, by K. S. Latourette. Copyright, 1948, by Harper & Brothers. Used by permission.

the Reformation imply that henceforth Protestantism has had a monopoly on the gospel. No such exclusive claim was ever made by the Reformers, and their doctrine of the invisible Church, as well as their explicit statements, made it clear that they were not excluding those whose faith and life were consciously grounded in the gospel. Just as there were evidences of the gospel in pre-Reformation times, so too in the post-Reformation period and continuing down to today there are "evangelical" Christians outside of Protestantism. In terms of the gospel, therefore, Protestantism is inclusive rather than exclusive.

An additional and very important distinction must be made, however. The Reformation, so we contend, was the rediscovery of the gospel, but it was not itself the gospel. The Reformation, in other words, was a historical interpretation of the gospel — revolutionary in its consequences but not perfect in its expression. Luther was clear about the gospel in terms of justification by faith, but ambiguous about the relation of Church and State. Calvin saw that the gospel could be expressed as a system of doctrine, but when he came to election and predestination, he was influenced by logic rather than the good news of God in Christ.

What is true of the Reformers themselves is even more obvious in the post-Reformation period. In the Lutheran and Reformed doctrinal disputes of the seventeenth and eighteenth centuries, the gospel is by no means self-evident. It is more apparent in such "reactionary" movements as Pietism in Germany, Wesleyanism in England, and the Great Awakening in America. The smaller sects, like the Anabaptists, Quakers, and Mennonites, frequently gave clearer expression to the gospel than the larger more established Protestant traditions. In other words, Protestantism is not to be thought of as a homogeneous illustration of the gospel. As in the Middle Ages, the gospel was never wholly lost, but it was never wholly present in all its power and relevance. And certainly the same could be said of contemporary Protestantism.

To speak of Protestantism as essential Christianity, therefore, is to speak of what Protestantism in its greatest moments has been and still can be. It is not, however, to claim more than history itself clearly teaches. All we can claim is that the gospel is what gives Protestantism its distinctively religious and Christian character. It is the gospel that animates doctrine, provokes preaching, and demands to be spread throughout the world. But just because the gospel is not always discernible in Protestant theology, preaching, and evangelism, it is possible to speak of the Reformation as incomplete or continuing.

What is the prospect for the future of Protestantism? Does the present confusion mean that the rediscovery of the Reformation has been lost? Are Protestantism's best years in the past? Is Protestantism a lifeless chrysalis, a dying cause, a backward look? Is this, in Paul Tillich's phrase, " the end of the Protestant era "? Have we evidence, on the other hand, to think that " the best is yet to be "? Is there reason to look forward to the continuation of the Reformation on a new scale and with renewed potency?

This much, at least, can be said, and it is a judgment based on faith and hope but it springs from the conviction that the revelation of God in Christ is for us and for our children: *The gospel is the secret to the tomorrow of Protestantism.* If for Protestantism the gospel becomes once more the good news of God in Christ, the future is bright with hope and promise. If, on the other hand, Protestantism should lose touch with the gospel, the prospect for Protestantism, no matter how energetic it may become, is gloomy indeed. The future of Protestantism does not depend upon the maintenance of the *status quo,* or upon radical emancipation from all the traditions of the past. It is not a matter of more theology or less theology, more liturgy or less liturgy, more organization or less organization. It will not be assured by retreats, or cells, or ecumenicity, or social action. It is quite simply and clearly a matter of witnessing to the gospel that God was in Christ for man's redemption. If this becomes the cornerstone of a future Protestantism, then theology, liturgy, organization, and all the rest can play their part — but without this nothing else will really matter. What such a Protestantism would be like in our time or in our children's time we cannot, of course, know. It might not even be called "Protestantism," and might conceivably be quite unrecognizable by modern standards.

What does it mean to say that Protestantism's fate hangs upon the gospel? This much we can say: It means that the gospel is not only the life, content, and dynamic of Protestantism, without which it must surely wither and die, but also that it is the norm, the standard, the judgment by which Protestantism is most radically challenged to be what it ought to be. We have spoken of the gospel as the informing principle of Protestant theology, preaching, and evangelism. Let us look to this other aspect of the matter and see how it is that the gospel calls Protestantism to task, judging its deficiencies, purging its aberrations and excesses, and setting before it a beacon and a summons. There are two broad areas where we may stake out the gospel claim to be norm and judge: the Church and individual Christian living.

FELLOWSHIP IN THE GOSPEL

Protestantism has often been accused of having no articulate doctrine of the Church, and this has generally been taken as a disastrous weakness. Romanism puts tne Church at the center of all its life and thought, and no Catholic is left in doubt as to what the Church is. Protestants, however, are embarrassed and bewildered by the obvious disunity of Churches and sects, which seems to negate any positive approach to a doctrine of the one, holy, catholic Church. The time has passed, if it ever really existed, when the church building could be identified with the Church, although doubtless many Protestants immediately think of their own local church or denomination when the word is mentioned. Protestant history, even the Reformation, does not seem to help toward a definition of the Church, for practically the whole range of ecclesiastical government and polity, from the Quaker meeting to the Anglo-Catholic insistence upon apostolic succession, has sprung from the same historical roots. Ecumenical gatherings have repeatedly addressed themselves to this question, but without appreciable effect upon the ingrained assumption that Protestantism has no doctrine of the Church, only doctrines of Churches.

The absence of a definite and definable doctrine of the Church is the result, first experienced in the Reformation and continuing until the present, of reaction to the medieval institutional and hierarchical structure. All Protestants unite, and have always united, in protesting against the ecclesiastical abuses of Rome. Even Anglo-Catholics, with all their deprecation of the Reformation and affinity for Rome, regard the papal system as untenable. In the process of retreating from the ecclesiastical tradition of the Roman Church, however, Protestantism has never been quite sure what to substitute for this repudiated doctrine of the Church. The stratagem of a visible and invisible Church was of little help, and Protestantism easily succumbed to the path of least resistance, which amounted to the creation of numerous ill-conceived Protestant institutions and organizations. Hence the Roman Catholic gibe that Protestantism left the one true Church for a multiplicity of lesser Churches, and in the process sold its birthright.

What appears to be an inherent weakness, however, may in fact be the suppressed remnant of a true Protestant instinct. The reaction against Roman ecclesiasticism was largely negative, but the negation implied, at least, a definite point of view, namely, that the Church is *not* an institutional structure such as Rome maintains. Some were more positive than this, and if Luther's unequivocal utterances, for example, had been taken seriously, Protestantism might have won through to a better end. One typical passage from the Reformer may be worth quoting at some length. It is from the essay entitled " On the Councils and the Churches " (1539), and Luther is referring to the article in the Apostles' Creed, " I believe in one holy Catholic [or ' Christian,' as he preferred] Church." He tells us that the New Testament word for Church, " *ecclesia*," simply means " a holy Christian people " gathered together by the Holy Spirit in the name of Christ. " If these words," he continues, " had been used in the Creed: ' I believe that there is a holy Christian people,' it would have been easy to avoid all the misery that has come in with this blind, obscure word ' church '; for the term ' Christian, holy people ' would have brought along with it, clearly and powerfully, both understanding and the judgment on the question ' What is and what is not a church? ' . . . *Ecclesia,* however, ought to mean the holy Christian people, not only of the time of the apostles, who are long since dead, but clear to the end of the world, so that there is always living on earth a Christian, holy people in which Christ lives, works, and reigns *per redemptionem,* through grace and forgiveness of sins, the Holy Ghost *per vivificationem et sanctificationem,* through the daily purging out of sins and renewal of life."

What Luther says here so clearly was for various reasons neglected and obscured in the subsequent Protestant development, partly perhaps because Luther himself later fell prey to the institutional definition of the Church. But the idea was not restricted to Luther and cropped out again and again, particularly among the smaller Reformation sects. What it implied was an entirely new interpretation of the Church, which on examination turns out to be not new at all but New Testament.

As Luther himself points out, the New Testament does not speak of the Church as an institution, a building, or an organization. It is always bound up with the idea of a called and gathered group of disciples who are what they are, namely, a Church, because of their common faith, common Lord, and common witness. The apostle Paul describes this " people " in several figures, the best known of which and the most suggestive being the " body " of Christ (I Cor., ch. 12, and elsewhere). It does not matter, for the moment, whether this figure be interpreted metaphorically, mystically, or realistically. All have been attempted, and Roman Catholics, Anglicans, sectarians, and others appeal to the idea for confirmation of their own views. What is important, however, is the obviously *personal* allusions that the figure has for the apostle's thought about the Church. The Church derives from Christ's body, which, we must remember, was the visible token of the incarnation, God in the flesh, the Eternal in a person. Thus it is possible to speak of the Church as the continuation of the incarnation. Now all this implies some sort of physical manifestation, just as Christ assumed a physical body for our redemption. But it would be a mistake and a misunderstanding of the figure to insist upon the form and character of this visible body to the utter exclusion of the personal relationship between Christ and his followers. It is the personal relationship, the fellowship, the mutual interdependence that constitutes the Church, whatever the nature of the visible structure may be.

The Reformation was aware of this New Testament view of the Church, but only dimly and unconsciously. Luther saw it, as the quotation just mentioned indicates, and the whole Protestant reaction to the Roman ecclesiastical institution implies it, but it never became a regnant principle as did, for example, the doctrine of justification by faith. In fact, as we have said, Protestantism slipped imperceptibly into a semi-Roman view of the Church, and it has never recovered the New Testament emphasis. In the post-Reformation period of the seventeenth and eighteenth centuries, the period of Protestant scholasticism, the personal character of the divine revelation was obscured by the development of a doctrinal confessionalism. Assent to correct doctrine was regarded as equivalent to personal faith in Christ. This meant that as doctrine came to be interpreted in terms of confessionalism and ethic in terms of legalism, so the Church, robbed of the personal fellowship emphasis, became increasingly thought of as an institution.

Protestantism's uneasiness about the doctrine of the Church is partly strength and partly weakness. It is strength in the sense that the Church is not a doctrine at all. It is not a "something" in which we believe. The New Testament never speaks of faith in the Church; it is always the fellowship of those who live in Christ, and never the object of faith. A doctrine of Christian fellowship has a cold and artificial sound; it makes the Church a "thing," an institution, a something to see and handle and manipulate. But the Church is simply Christ living in his people. This is, of course, visible, just as true friendship or love is visible, but the bond of fellowship is invisible or personal. Wherever there has been a self-conscious Protestant doctrine of the Church, this personal relationship between Christ and his people has been emphasized. The Protestant interpretation of the body of Christ is in terms of spiritual life, not ecclesiastical anatomy. That does not mean that there is no physical or institutional reality known as the Church, but that the essence of the Church, which gives the physical body its soul and life, is the Christian fellowship of the communion of saints.

The weakness of the Protestant view has been simply its inability to steer a middle course between a mystical and an institutional conception of the Church. The one stresses the New Testament note of fellowship but fails to make the fellowship visible; the other is so concerned with the visible reality that the personal element is obscured. Thus Protestantism has been rent asunder by sects of all kinds, which have been separatist in the sense of withdrawing from the cold formality of a Protestant institutionalism, and by Churches that feel that their form of government, their view of the ministry, their view of worship must be maintained at all costs. The one forgets that the body of Christ is in the flesh, incarnation. The other forgets that " it is the spirit that gives life."

This inner conflict in the Protestant view of the Church is perhaps inevitable and beyond any easy resolution. It is the conflict between soul and body, spirit and matter; it is the sacramental principle that defies rigidity and fixity. But the tension could surely be eased if both views were to appeal to the New Testament emphasis of the Church as the gathered people of God in Christ. And it is just here that the gospel becomes not only life and content but norm and judge. The gospel is the good news of God in Christ for man's redemption. This definition is made up of personal terms. It is not a doctrine or an event or a thing — it is the personal relation between God and Christ and mankind. If this gospel note could be sounded in all our thinking about the Church, the present confusion and ambiguity — to say nothing of the petty bickering and animosity — could be transcended.

Furthermore, the idea of fellowship itself is deepened and clarified by reference to the gospel. The Church is a fellowship not merely in the sense in which a club or fraternal organization is a gathering together of like-minded people. The Church is a fellowship *in the gospel*. Many efforts are made in our day to re-create fellowship within the Church, but often this is done under the illusion that if only people can be induced to come into the church building, whether for supper, games, cards, dancing, bazaars, or what not, then a sense of fellowship will follow. That may indeed be the case, and there are numerous examples of what are generally regarded as active and vital churches that run a full schedule of meetings and activities of all sorts throughout the week. But the Church is fellowship, not for its own sake or for the sake of mutual entertainment or even uplift; it is quite specifically fellowship in the gospel. It is the awareness of a new common life which has its source in the good news about God in Christ. Such a fellowship may find expression in all kinds of social activities as well as in common worship, but it is a mark of our misunderstanding of the New Testament conception of the Church when we think that we can have the fellowship without the gospel.

The gospel calls us back in our view of the Church to Christ and his life in us. This would not preclude a doctrine of the visible Church, the ministry, the sacraments, government, and all the rest, but it would infuse a new sense of meaning into all our discussions. The Church would become the incarnation in history of the gospel. It would give free and personal expression to the good news that in Christ a new sense of human and divine togetherness is possible. It would undergird the ministry with a divine commission to keep the fellowship in the gospel alive. It would infuse the worship of the Church, whether in preaching, liturgy, or sacrament, with a divine purpose. The government of the Church, programs of religious education, evangelistic activities, ecumenical consciousness, and social concern would all become visible expressions and illustrations of the fact of Christian fellowship in Christ. All this might not appreciably change the present structure of Protestantism, but it would mean a virtual resurrection from the dead. The dry bones would be clothed upon with sinew and muscle, and the breath of God would animate the body with a living soul. Ezekiel's vision (ch. 37) came in a time of despair and uncertainty. It was a summons to faith and hope and a prophecy for the future. The gospel repeats the challenge for our day, and the future of the Protestant Church hangs in the balance.

WHAT IT MEANS TO BE A CHRISTIAN

If the Protestant conception of the Church has been stripped of the New Testament emphasis upon the members and the body of Christ, the reason may not be far to seek. How can there be a sense of togetherness, a communion of saints, a mutual ministry in the Lord, if there are so few who know what this means in personal individual experience? If the fellowship does not already exist in some real and vital way, it cannot be compounded out of synthetic longings and wistful hopes. If the fellowship does exist and takes some visible and tangible form, then an outsider may sense that there is an invisible bond that accounts for this, and he may seek to learn more about it through association. But that is where Protestantism is weakest. Ministers as a rule are not deluged with requests from outsiders to " join " the Church because they want to have a part in the Church's vital spirit of fellowship. They may " join " for a variety of reasons, some good and some not so good, and most ministers are so glad to get them on any terms that few questions are asked. But the Church is not the voluntary association of people who get together to form a fellowship. It is not a society of respectable spectators. The Church *is* the fellowship, and if the fellowship does not exist, the Church ceases to be the incarnation of the good news and becomes a club, an organization for mutual uplift, a *place* to worship and meditate.

If there are few in our Churches who know at first hand what the gospel is, it is unlikely that the Church will be a fellowship in the gospel. That is why individual Churches may have large " enrollments " and yet at the same time give little evidence of the power of the gospel in thought, life, and action. Protestantism has been proceeding on the mistaken formula that if only enough people can be brought into the Churches, the New Testament fellowship will follow as a natural consequence. But the fellowship is the communion of those who have heard the good news of the gospel and have responded in full commitment and self-dedication. The fellowship does not come into being in any other way, and the fellowship *is* the Church.

All this raises the question of what it means to be a Christian. Kierkegaard defined the Christian as one who lives as if Christ were a contemporary, and who is and acts as the disciples who followed their Lord even in his humiliation and rejection. There is nothing original about this definition except for the last phrase. Others have defined the Christian as one who walks with Christ. But Kierkegaard's definition goes beyond contemporaneousness with Christ to insist that such a personal relationship involves *offense*. It means associating with one who was despised and rejected by men. It means following in the footsteps of one whose path led to a cross and who asked his disciples to take up their own cross.

Nothing is gained by playing down the costliness of Christian discipleship. Jesus never slurred over the demands that his summons, " Follow me," involved. The disciples literally gave up everything. The Gentile converts were aware that they were associating themselves with a people whose history had been one long experience in suffering, persecution, and exile. The Christians of the Early Church knew that their faith could be tested in the arena and that martyrdom was an ever-present possibility. This is the " offense " of being a Christian, and it is something of which modern Christians do not like to be reminded. To be a Christian in the modern sense means to adopt the " high " ethical values of the teaching of Jesus. It means appropriating Jesus' way of gentleness and compassion. It means standing for the best in our Christian culture and civilization. That is why Kierkegaard could say, " Christendom has done away with Christianity, without being quite aware of it."

If this severe and rigid definition of what it means to be a Christian is not overdrawn, is it any wonder that the witness of Protestantism languishes and the fellowship of the Church is so weak and feeble? Is not time for the Church to be honest and forthright about the difficulty of being a Christian? What would happen if this definition of a Christian became the prerequisite for membership in the Church? The immediate reaction would be apparent catastrophe.

Churches would be emptied and rolls depleted overnight if this sort of loyalty test were exacted. But would the Church succumb?

Such a decimation and liquidation of the ranks is perhaps too drastic. But either the Church must be clear in its preaching and teaching regarding the costs of Christian discipleship or one of two alternatives, perhaps both, will confront us. Either the Church will continue on its present ineffectual way, unaware that it is no longer the Church, or groups of individuals here and there will secede from the lifeless corpse and the Church will appear in most unlikely places and among most unlikely people. The gospel is at work in the world, and if Protestantism does not put itself under its power and judgment, it will break out somewhere else.

What, we may ask, does the gospel have to do with this conception of what it means to be a Christian? Have we not been at pains to emphasize the element of good news, joy, hope, gladness, and victory? Where does this fit in with the demand for identification with Christ's humiliation and rejection? Suppose we ask those who knew something about this. Here is Paul: "Therefore, since we are justified by faith, we have peace with God through our Lord Jesus Christ . . . and we rejoice in our hope of sharing the glory of God. More than that, we rejoice in our sufferings" (Rom. 5:1-3). Here is James: "Count it all joy, my brethren, when you meet various trials" (James 1:2). Here is Peter: "Blessed be the God and Father of our Lord Jesus Christ! . . . In this you rejoice, though now for a little while you may have to suffer various trials" (I Peter 1:3, 6).

The gospel is the good news, not that life will be made easy, not that the Christian will be spared all "the slings and arrows of outrageous fortune," but that God in Christ has triumphed. This is good news in temptation, joy in suffering, rejoicing in trials. It is the good news that only the committed Christian can hope to know. It is the joy that cancels the offense. It is the gladness that binds all Christians together and ties them into the fellowship of the Church.

Far from enervating the life and activity of the Church, the recapture of the gospel in all its stringency and demand would unquestionably become its most potent means of new life and evangelism. Serious-thinking people are not fooled for long by a gospel that cannot face up to the tragedies and realities of life. Young people today will not enlist in a cause that makes no demands or waters down the deep issues of life and existence. The Church will be the Church when it dares to proclaim the eternal gospel without fear or favor.

THE CONSUMMATION OF PROTESTANTISM

When we speak of the tomorrow of Protestantism, we do not merely raise the question about its possible survival in the next few years or even generations. It seems likely that as a spiritual and religious influence, as an organized movement, as a sociological phenomenon, Protestantism is sure to persist for some time to come. There is no immediate danger that it will suddenly cease to be or that it will be forced to abdicate its place within the structure of the modern world. But that is small comfort for Protestantism's uneasy conscience. The tomorrow for which we look is not a mere continuance of things as they are but the dawning of a new day which will bring with it possibilities of a re-creative dynamic.

If there is to be a tomorrow of Protestantism in this sense, it will be born of radical repentance. If contemporary confusion is to give way to a positive Protestantism, there must be a sense of present inadequacy and insufficiency. It is not enough to look forward to the continuing existence of Protestantism as we now know it. Something must happen to its very soul if it is to be reborn and live anew.

It is the great strength of Protestantism that it can think of itself as subject to the call of repentance. The inner principle of protest which demands that Protestantism be self-critical and therefore self-conscious of its own deficiencies is the basis of hope for anticipating a tomorrow that will provide opportunities to amend its ways and to reassert and reaffirm its essential nature. If this tomorrow, therefore, is not to be just another day, it must be approached with contrition and shame for the sins of the past, together with the determination to step over the threshold of the future with a renewed conviction of prophetic mission and evangelical commitment.

This penitent but expectant attitude toward tomorrow illustrates in a clear and forceful way the essential difference between Protestantism and Roman Catholicism. Both are concerned and agitated about the future but for very different reasons, and with quite distinct presuppositions about what tomorrow may bring. Romanism looks forward to the further expansion and extension of its own highly developed structure. It is at the moment convinced that a life-and-death struggle is being waged between Catholicism and Communism, and the tomorrow of Romanism is envisaged as the complete and utter defeat of what it takes to be its most formidable competitor. In all this, however, there is not the slightest shred of evidence that the Roman Church is *self*-critical or in any way itself subject to the call of repentance and reformation.

Protestantism differs from Romanism in its anticipation of

tomorrow by taking seriously the apostolic injunction that "judgment must begin at the house of God" (I Peter 4:17). To be sure, Protestantism has not always shown itself ready to accept this divine judgment and has frequently given little evidence of responding to it, but at the present time there is a growing realization that something radical, revolutionary, and prophetic must lay hold of Protestantism if it is to meet the future unafraid. The Reformation dictum that the church needs always to be reformed (*Ecclesia semper reformari debet*) is being invoked with a renewed sense of urgency in our day, and the measure in which this challenge is accepted indicates not only the radical difference between Protestantism and Romanism but also the only ground for looking forward toward the future with hope and promise.

The judgment with which the Christian Church is always confronted is, quite simply, the gospel. The Church is truly the Church whenever the gospel is made the content and norm of its faith and life. And if the gospel is absent or obscured, the Church cannot really be the Church. Romanism is as much under the judgment of the gospel as Protestantism, perhaps more so since it tends to judge that which really judges it. But our concern is with Protestantism, and here there can be no question that if there is to be a tomorrow of Protestantism, the judgment of the gospel must be recognized and acknowledged.

If once more Protestantism can unfurl the gospel of God's love for man in Jesus Christ as its crusading banner, it will not need to fear tomorrow but will be ready for what is to come with a sense of divine commission and holy purpose. It would be futile to predict what form such a new evangelicalism would assume. That would be to anticipate our response to the gospel and the free work of God's Spirit in us. Our first responsibility is to be aware of what the gospel is and what it has to say to us, for only as we are sure of this can we hope for the emergence of a positive Protestantism. Such a Protestantism may well be so radically different from what we now know as Protestantism that the name itself may become ambiguous and misleading. That is nothing to fear, and perhaps would be evidence that the gospel had begun its work in us. And if theology, preaching, evangelism, ethics, and the Church could all be brought under the judgment of the gospel, there is no doubt that old things would be done away and all things would become new. It is only through such a re-creation that there is hope, not only for Protestantism, but for the whole of Christendom.

It is here that Protestantism has set before it not only its great opportunity but also its staggering and superlative responsibility. For the tomorrow of Protestantism is not an end in itself, but only a means to an end, namely, to make the gospel regnant in the faith and life of the Christian Church. The future to which we look, therefore, is no sectarian expansion of Protestantism as we now know it. In this sense, the tomorrow of Protestantism may well mean the end of Protestantism. The cause for which we fight and the victory for which we strive is not Protestantism but Christianity.

Nevertheless Protestantism has a destiny to act as the evangelical conscience of Christendom, recalling itself and all other forms of the Christian faith back to the gospel of God in Christ. It is simply a matter of fact that at the present time neither Romanism nor Eastern Orthodoxy can perform this work of evangelical revival, for neither is willing to subject itself to the divine judgment of the gospel. It is not certain that Protestantism will succeed, but at the present moment, as we stand poised on the brink of the future, Protestantism seems to be providentially confronted with the supreme mission of reaffirming for the Christian Church the good news of what God has done for man in Jesus Christ.

If Protestantism will commit itself in an act of self-dedication to the consummation of this divine commission, the tomorrow of Protestantism will involve not only self-renunciation but self-realization. To this end Protestantism must apply to itself the repeated warning of the Lord to his disciples: " Whoever would save his life will lose it; and whoever loses his life for my sake and the gospel's will save it " (Mark 8:35).

Date Due
